Georgiana 'Browning' Hill was the author of a number of cookery books in the late 1800s, which include *The Gourmet's Guide to Rabbit Cooking*, published in 1859, *The Breakfast Book*, published in 1865, and *How to Cook Apples*, published in 1865. Her popular early cookbooks offered simple food for the middle classes and sold at sixpence each. She enjoyed success with her later titles, which became more adventurous, with recipes from Spain and France, and were aimed at more serious gourmets. The dates of her birth and death are unknown.

A Year of Victorian Puddings was originally published as *Everybody's Pudding Book* in 1862.

A
YEAR OF
VICTORIAN
PUDDINGS

Traditional Tarts, Pies and Puddings
for Every Day of the Year

GEORGIANA HILL

MACMILLAN

First published as *Everybody's Pudding Book* in 1862 by Richard Bentley & Son

This edition published as *A Year of Victorian Puddings* in 2012 by Macmillan
an imprint of Pan Macmillan, a division of Macmillan Publishers Limited
Pan Macmillan, 20 New Wharf Road, London N1 9RR
Basingstoke and Oxford
Associated companies throughout the world
www.panmacmillan.com

ISBN 978-0-230-76782-9

Visit www.panmacmillan.com to read more about all our books
and to buy them. You will also find features, author interviews and
news of any author events, and you can sign up for e-newsletters
so that you're always first to hear about our new releases.

CONTENTS.

INTRODUCTION.

"You appear very partial to apple puddings," I observed to an elderly lady, with whose family I had been staying during the greater part of a dull November, and had been surprised to find that I had been uninterruptedly regaled upon the dish in question for the whole time of my visit.

"Partial to apple puddings?" she replied, drearily, "no, indeed, I am not; but of all the troubles in life entailed by housekeeping, that of having daily to appoint the pies or puddings proper for the season is the worst; so, after mature reflection, I determined rather than to attempt evading the annoyance by seeking refuge in a boarding-house, or taking to travelling, to adopt the easier expedient of insisting upon my cook's confining herself entirely to providing me with apple puddings for one half the year, and gooseberry puddings for the other half: so if I can persuade you to remain with us till May, you can then count upon a change; but in the interim you may expect nothing but the appearance of these inevitable apple puddings, and from Whitsuntide to the feast of the Assumption, as reasonably rely upon their being replaced by puddings of gooseberry. I cannot say I quite approve of the arrangement now I have tried it, but at all events," she added, looking ruefully at the insipid preparation of pastry before her, "I believe I am getting reconciled to it by degrees, for only think the world of altercation, anxiety, and contrivance it has exempted me from!"

This slight incident decided me to undertake a work for the assistance and enlightenment of any ladies who may be in like distress; and if through my editorial exertions, one of the fair or even sterner sex be spared a moment's trouble upon the subject (for creation's lords do dabble in dinners somewhat), or one superfluous pudding, whether of apple or of gooseberry, be spared society, I shall not only, as common cant would say, consider myself amply rewarded, but feel I am incontestably entitled to be looked upon as a benefactor of my species. And with all the sincerity of an epicure, I hope that, with this manual to consult, no one will be any longer at a loss what to order or what to have.

Besides puddings, tarts, and pies, I have introduced custards, not that they can be considered as coming under the category of pastry, but on account of their being essential additions to many kinds of tarts and fruit-puddings, and likewise form an agreeable variety upon the dinner-table.

Fritters, omelettes, and other entremets, I have also given, because they are quickly made, and I know from experience that nothing is more difficult than for a housekeeper to make choice of an easily-prepared dish of pastry upon occasions of emergency, when suddenly called upon to produce a dinner for unexpected visitors.

I may add that in compiling this work it has not been my aim to make a mere collection of all the puddings ever known; there are many very worthy compositions, such as pies of parsley, tarts of cabbage, puddings of leeks, and others of that sort that I have purposely omitted, feeling convinced that although these dishes were locally esteemed, they would be scarcely likely to meet with popular acceptance.

Where I have named any particular pudding twice, it will be seen that there exists an important difference, not only in the manner of making it, but in the mode of its being cooked—in the one case boiling, and in the other case baking being necessary; and although many of the fresh fruit-tarts and puddings I have mentioned are almost similarly prepared, I have preferred treating each in its appointed place rather than subject my readers to the annoyance of seeking for a dish and only finding it included under a general heading, and even then, perhaps, being referred to another chapter for further instructions respecting it.

The quantities of the ingredients in the several compositions here given will be found to be proportioned to the requirements of a small family; and though at first sight some of the dishes may not be thought to be of a recherché description, yet the majority of them is highly so; and while the humblest of the preparations presented in these pages will, upon trial, be found to have merited their well-established reputations for homely excellence, the more elegant amongst them also possess the one great recommendation of being within the reach of Amphitryons and housekeepers of the most moderate means.

BROWNING HILL,
January, 1862.

JANUARY.

THE return of January invariably appears to bring with it the ratification of all the bright hopes of enjoyment which arose in our hearts at the approach of Christmas: in January, above any other period of the year, the interchange of hospitality between friends takes place, and if any difficulty is experienced as to the provisions to be made for the entertainment of our guests, as far as pastry is concerned, it proceeds from the embarrassment occasioned by the extensive variety of the good things at our command, rather than from any existing paucity of materials; for notwithstanding it is midwinter-time, and fresh fruits of home production are comparatively scarce, yet pears, apples, and medlars can still be procured, and these, too, in tolerable flavour and condition, while lemons, oranges, nuts, almonds, etc., are in abundance; and, besides the tempting displays of raisins, currants, candied-peels, and spices offered to our notice by the importers of foreign fruits, the shelves of all good housekeepers should still be stored with a fair share of preserves of different descriptions, which, with the numerous farinaceous substances, such as sago, tapioca, rice, and others that are always readily obtained, our resources of festivity will be found to be most ample. Certainly it is not a favourable time for milk, cream, and butter—and eggs are as yet far from plentiful; but then beef-suet and sweet hogs'-lard are in the height of their perfection, and with these essential adjuncts, and good flour at our disposal, the production of admirable pastry may be assured, providing always that proper care is bestowed upon the manner in which these ingredients be employed: and here I must remark that a well-made crust, whether for tart, pie, or pudding, will make almost any preparation of pastry worthy of commendation; and if the directions given for crust-making be attentively adhered to, and your cook possess the indispensable qualifications of *cleanliness* and *quickness*, the success of your pastry may be pretty safely depended upon.

PLAIN SUET CRUST FOR BOILED PUDDINGS.

Eight ounces of chopped beef-suet, a small spoonful of salt, and twelve ounces of dry flour, mixed well together, and kneaded with a sufficiency of cold water, and rolled out to fit your basin as required, will be found enough for what is called a quart pudding. Suet crusts are generally preferred for boiled puddings and dumplings, as when lard or butter is used, the paste is apt to look dark coloured when dressed.

BUTTER CRUST FOR BOILED PUDDINGS.

Rather less butter or lard answers for a boiled crust, or it gets soft in the course of cooking, and is likely to allow the juices of the pudding to escape; six ounces of either lard or butter to ten ounces of flour will be sufficient. Add a little salt; rub the fat well into the flour, then put water enough to form a light but not a too moist paste. If, however, a greater degree of richness be desired, more fat may be employed, but two well-beaten eggs should then be added to give consistency to the crust. This kind of paste is principally used for convenience as a substitute for suet crust when suet is not to be had.

Remember solid puddings, such as those composed of fresh fruit, and Christmas puddings, require to be boiled for at least one hour for every pound weight of the pudding: soft puddings of the custard or bread kind need less cooking.

TART OR PIE CRUST.

Every housekeeper has her own particular way of making puff-pastes, pie-crusts, etc.; but, as a rule, half a pound of butter or lard to one pound of flour will be sufficiently rich for family purposes—these being either mixed by first working in a portion of the butter with the greater part of the flour, then adding a very little water, and finishing by rolling out the paste very thin and applying the remaining butter and dredging in the rest of the flour, then folding it up and rolling it until of the necessary thickness; or, most of the flour may be made into a very stiff paste with a little water and the beaten white of an egg, afterwards repeatedly rolled out and buttered and dredged with flour until the requisite weight of each be employed. For very light crusts, a small quantity of sugar is added, and more butter is allowed— sometimes in an equal proportion to the flour; but in making paste for fresh fruit tarts no sugar should be used, as the steam rising and condensing in cooking makes the crust eat limp and tough. Remember, for all kinds of baking, the heat of the oven should be what the French call *gay*, but on no account violent.

And now, since we cannot be profuse in our employment of eggs this month, we will select only those puddings and tarts in the composition of which eggs either do not enter, or are at least but sparingly required.

PUDDINGS, ETC., FOR JANUARY.

Swiss Pudding.

Cheap Plum Pudding.

Winter Apple Pie.

Currant Fritters without Eggs.

Millet Pudding.

Lemon Dumplings.

A Spoonful Pudding.

Medlar Tart.

Suet Dumplings with Currants.

Madeira Pudding.

Quick-made Pudding.

Bread-and-butter Pudding, baked.

Batter Pudding without Eggs.

Snowballs.

Orange Tart.

Curd Puddings.

Raspberry Dumplings.

Small Citron Puddings.

Flour Hasty Pudding.

Milk Custards.

Lemon Ratafia Pudding.

Plum Pudding without Eggs.

The Portland Pudding.

Common Currant Dumplings.

SWISS PUDDING.

Take a pint each of fine bread-crumbs and minced apples, put them in alternate layers into a well-buttered pie-dish, with a sprinkling of chopped blanched almonds, currants, and sugar between each layer. When you have placed in all the ingredients, pour in six ounces of fresh butter previously melted, dust over the top with more bread-crumbs, and bake it for half an hour.

CHEAP PLUM PUDDING.

Take half a pound each of shred suet and fine flour, a quarter of a pound of carefully-washed currants, a teaspoonful of spice, a little lemon-peel grated, a dessert-spoonful of sugar, one egg, and enough milk to make it into a stiff batter. Tie it in a cloth, and boil it for two hours. This little pudding will not cost you a shilling, and will be found exceedingly good.

WINTER APPLE PIE.

Line the rim of your pie-dish with puff-paste, then pare, core, and cut up half a dozen apples; mix them with the juice of a lemon and a little of the grated rind, half a pound of cleaned currants, a quarter of a pound of white sugar, and a quarter of a pound of sliced fresh butter; lay this into your pie-dish, cover it with a delicate thin crust, and bake it for an hour.

CURRANT FRITTERS WITHOUT EGGS.

Take half a pint of mild Scotch ale, gradually stir flour into it until it forms a tolerably thick but smooth batter. Beat it up very briskly, and add an ounce of cleaned and dried currants. When your frying-pan of boiling lard is ready, put in a spoonful at a time here and there until the pan is covered with fritters; shake them that they may not catch, and when they are beautifully browned on both sides, take them up and serve with lemon-juice and sifted white sugar.

MILLET PUDDING.

Take a quarter of a pound of millet-seed; pick it over and wash it carefully; then mix it with a quarter of a pound of sugar and half a grated nutmeg. Put it into a well-buttered pie-dish, and pour over it a quart of warmed milk in which two ounces of fresh butter have been melted. Bake it until the seed is quite soft, and serve hot.—N.B. If possible, skim-milk should be used, so as to bring the expense of this dish to about sixpence; for no "milky pudding" for family purposes is worth more.

LEMON DUMPLINGS.

Take a quarter of a pound each of chopped beef-suet, pounded loaf-sugar, and stale bread-crumbs, the juice and shred rind of a lemon, an egg beaten up in a dessert-spoonful of brandy, and a little powdered ginger; mix all well together, divide it into four dumplings, wrap each in a floured cloth, and boil for twenty minutes. Serve with sweet sauce over them.

A SPOONFUL PUDDING.

Take a tablespoonful each of flour and milk—or cream if you have it—one egg, a saltspoonful each of ginger, nutmeg, and salt, and a dessert-spoonful of currants, well washed, and afterwards dried in a cloth. Mix these things well together, and either put it into a small basin and boil, or bake it in a tart-mould. Half an hour will do it.

MEDLAR TART.

Slightly bruise a dozen medlars, and put them into a pie-dish, with four dessert-spoonsful of pounded loaf-sugar and a quart of sweet cider; let them bake slowly until the liquor is a syrup; then pulp the medlars through a sieve; add more sugar to the syrup; mix it with the fruit: line the edge of a tart-dish with a puff-paste; put in your medlars; cover with a top crust, and bake for half an hour in a moderate oven.

SUET DUMPLINGS WITH CURRANTS.

Scald a pint of new milk, and let it grow cold; then stir into it a pound of chopped suet, two eggs, four ounces of cleaned currants, a little nutmeg and salt, two teaspoonsful of powdered ginger, and flour sufficient to make the whole into a light batter-paste. Form it into dumplings, flour them well outside, throw them into your saucepan, being careful that the water is boiling, and that they do not stick to the bottom. Half an hour's boiling will do them.

MADEIRA PUDDING.

Take a tin cake-mould, butter it very well inside, and cover the bottom of it with a piece of fine puff-paste; over this put a layer of pineapple-jam, then another layer of paste, then another of preserve, if possible varying it by using apricot-jam or quince-marmalade: proceed thus with alternate layers of fruit and paste until the whole is full, observing to finish with a layer of paste. Tie it down with a well-floured cloth, and boil it for three hours. Turn it out carefully, and serve with brandy sauce.

A QUICK-MADE PUDDING.

Take two ounces of grated bread-crumbs, four ounces each of chopped suet and flour, two eggs, two ounces of sultana raisins, two ounces of currants washed and dried, and a little sugar and spice: mix the whole well together with a breakfast-cupful of new milk; put it into a floured cloth, and boil it for thirty minutes.

This pudding is easily made, inexpensive, and very good. Serve it with lemon or wine sauce.

BREAD-AND-BUTTER PUDDING, BAKED.

Cut some very thin slices of bread and butter, lay them in a well-buttered pie-dish, interspersing them with a sprinkling of currants very carefully washed and picked, a little powdered sugar, and some finely-shred lemon-peel; then make a custard by boiling two bruised laurel-leaves in a pint of milk; remove them, gradually beat two eggs into the milk, pour it over the bread, let it remain two hours to soak, and afterwards bake it for half an hour in a pretty quick oven.

Some people prefer having the edge of the dish lined with a rim of very light paste. This can be had or omitted, according to taste; but the look of most baked puddings is much improved by the addition of an edge of crust boldly notched.

BATTER PUDDING WITHOUT EGGS.

By degrees mix four dessert-spoonsful of flour into a pint of new milk; add two teaspoonsful each of ginger and strong tincture of saffron, a salt-spoonful of salt, and two dessert-spoonsful of sultana raisins, previously swelled in brandy. Put it into a cloth or buttered basin, and boil it an hour. Serve either with plain melted butter or sweet sauce. Batter puddings of all kinds should be moved about a little after they are put into the boiling water, to prevent the ingredients from separating and settling at the bottom.

SNOWBALLS.

Take half a pound of the best rice, put it into a saucepan with a quart of new milk; simmer it slowly, so that it may not burn: when it has absorbed all the milk, let it cool; then mix in the whites of two eggs; pare and core some middling-sized apples; put a little sugar into each, then envelope them in rice: tie them in cloths, and boil them for twenty minutes or half an hour, according to the quality of the apples used. Turn them into a dish to serve, and dust them thickly over with loaf-sugar.

The advantage of this dish is that it employs the whites of eggs; and sometimes, after making custards or preparations which require the yolks of eggs, housekeepers are at a loss how to turn the whites to account.

ORANGE TART.

Take the juice and pulp of four oranges, either Seville or the common kind, and the rind of one pared as thinly as possible, and cut into little snips; work them thoroughly together with half a pound of refined sugar, two beaten eggs, a glass of French brandy, two ounces of butter, and two ounces of pounded and sifted biscuit: completely line a tart-dish with a very fine puff-paste; lay in the ingredients, and bake for twenty minutes in a moderate oven. When eaten cold, some rich cream may be poured over the top before sending to table, which will greatly increase its richness.

CURD PUDDINGS.

Take a good pint of curds well pressed from the whey; rub them through a sieve; add the crumb of two penny rolls, a grated nutmeg, six ounces of butter first melted, a teacupful of cream, and enough sugar to sweeten it: work it well together with a spoon; butter the insides of small pudding-cups, three parts fill them with the mixture, and bake them for ten minutes or a quarter of an hour. Serve them in the cups, or turn them into a dish, as you fancy.

RASPBERRY DUMPLINGS.

Make a good suet crust as for a pudding, roll it out, but not too thin, spread it over with raspberry-jam, roll it up, tie it in a cloth, and boil it for an hour. When done, cut it into five pieces, pour melted butter into the dish, and strew the dumplings thickly over with sifted loaf-sugar.

If preferred, you can make the crust with lard or butter, add your jam, and simply bake in a moderately-heated oven.

SMALL CITRON PUDDINGS.

Mix well together a tablespoonful of fine dry flour, two ounces of pounded loaf-sugar, half a grated nutmeg, half a pint of new milk or cream, two ounces of candied citron-peel cut exceedingly thin, and the yolks of two eggs; put it into small buttered cups, bake them in a tolerably brisk oven for a quarter of an hour, and turn into a dish to serve.

FLOUR HASTY-PUDDING.

Bruise four bay-leaves, and boil them in a quart of milk; when they have boiled a few minutes, remove them, and having beaten up the yolks of two eggs in a few spoonsful of cold milk, stir them gradually into the boiling milk; then take a dredger, and, still stirring with one hand, dredge in some flour, until you have a smooth batter of good thickness; let it come to a boil, and continue stirring it all the time; then pour it into your dish, and slice butter over the top. Add sugar, and serve. The eggs may be omitted if they cannot be obtained; but they are a considerable improvement to the pudding.

MILK CUSTARDS.

Take a pint of the afterings, or last milkings from the cow, set it upon the fire with a little cinnamon or two laurel-leaves; when it begins to boil take it off, and, having well mixed a tablespoon-ful each of flour and thick cream, strain the hot milk slowly upon them, stirring steadily as you do so: work it very smooth, sweeten to the taste, and bake it either in cups or patty-pans lined with paste.

LEMON RATAFIA PUDDING.

Boil the finely-shred peel of six lemons until it is quite soft, then take it up and pound it in a mortar; add a quarter of a pound of butter first melted, four ratafia cakes, the juice of two lemons, the yolks of five eggs, and the whites of three: mix all well together; sweeten to your taste; put in a glass of brandy; lay it in a shallow dish lined with puff-paste, and bake slowly for forty minutes.

PLUM PUDDING WITHOUT EGGS.

Take one pound of shred beef-suet, one pound of flour, three-quarters of a pound each of stoned raisins and washed currants, half a pound of bread-crumbs, two tablespoonsful of sugar, a little grated lemon-peel, a dessert-spoonful of ground ginger, and half a pint of milk or water to mix it with. Boil it for six hours in a floured cloth. Serve with wine-sauce.

THE PORTLAND PUDDING.

Well beat the yolks and whites of four eggs, add to them one tablespoonful each of flour and sugar, a pound of raisins, and a pound of veal-suet; mix the whole well together; put it into a buttered basin; tie it well down with a floured cloth, and boil it for five hours. Serve with sauce poured into the dish.

COMMON CURRANT DUMPLINGS.

These are made with some plain suet-paste into which are sprinkled some cleaned dried currants, in the proportion of two ounces of currants to a pound of paste: too many currants make the dumplings heavy. Boil them half an hour.

FEBRUARY.

INDEPENDENTLY of "Spring pies," by which dish February is generally distinguished, this month most frequently ushers in Shrovetide, and on one day at least, in the course of the year, we need be in no doubt as to what we are to have for dinner—on Shrove Tuesday, golden-hued, tender, savoury pancakes are indispensable; they have become almost an institution of our country—an institution it were *lèze-majesté* not to respect and properly maintain. We may shirk our saffron cakes at Easter, we may ignore all pastry responsibilities at Middle Lent; may honourably escape from the obligation of having a goose at Michaelmas; nay, even, pretermit our pudding at Christmas, by making a mean compromise with mince-pies; but to pass by Pancake Day without duly furnishing and partaking of the old familiar fare prescribed for the occasion, would be something of an unorthodoxy, unheard of—an enormity of wickedness likely to bring down the most dire calamity upon the head of him or her so offending: for if it is implicitly believed that the very venial sin of tasting soup at Easter is visited by the infliction of a cold in the head for a whole year after, how much more terrible must the retribution that awaits the bad-living wretch who wilfully and deliberately abstains from the time-honoured dish ordained for this day! And next to the fate attending those who are insensible to the importance of eating pancakes, may the severest misfortunes befall all who bring them into disrepute by preparing them badly; for though I have called pancakes golden-hued, and tender, and savoury, they are oftener so hard, so heavy, so scorched and greasy, that conscientious gourmets are fully justified in declining to touch them; and the reason of this proceeds from the persistence of English cooks in indiscriminately making use of both whites and yolks of the eggs, instead of the yolks only, which should alone be employed; besides this, they persevere in frying our pancakes in butter or dripping, and do not care much whether this boils before putting in the batter. Now, next to lard or oil, a French friture should be preferred for frying pastry; this should be made by melting down equal parts of the loin fat of beef, pork, and veal, straining it off and keeping it in jars until wanted.

PUDDINGS, ETC., FOR FEBRUARY.

Easy-made Pudding.
Crêpes, or French Pancakes.
The Bakewell Pudding.
Cream Pancakes.
Rhubarb Tart, or Spring Pie.
Plain Custards.
Raisin Pudding.
Lemon Cheesecakes.
Persian Pudding.
Almond Tarts.
Prune Pudding.
Plain Suet Dumplings.

Transparent Pudding.
Orange Custards.
Bread Pudding, boiled.
Hasty Fritters.
The Buckingham Pudding.
The Prior's Pudding.
Family Rice Pudding, baked.
Plum Pudding, baked.
New College Pudding, boiled.
Pound Pudding.
Chocolate Tart.
Milk Pancakes.

EASY-MADE PUDDING.

Take half a pound each of currants, flour, and chopped beef-suet, four ounces of treacle, and a breakfast-cupful of milk; add a little spice; mix well together, and boil it in a cloth or basin for four hours.

CRÊPES, OR FRENCH PANCAKES.

Well beat the yolks of four eggs, mix them into a pound of flour; add a glass of brandy, and with an equal quantity of good ale and water dilute the paste until it is of the consistency of cream; let this remain for two hours before using, then put a piece of friture as large as a walnut into the frying-pan; hold it over a clear fire until it smokes; put in enough batter to cover the bottom of the pan, and when nicely browned on one side, turn it, and as soon as it is done, serve with lemon, ginger-sauce, or spiced sugar apart. Put in another piece of friture for each succeeding pancake you have to fry.

THE BAKEWELL PUDDING.

Make a very rich pie-crust, and with it line the inside of a tart-dish; then spread over it a thick layer of preserved cherries, jam, or marmalade of any kind. Make a composition with the beaten yolks of four and the whites of two very fresh eggs, a quarter of a pound of powdered and sifted white sugar, a quarter of a pound of butter melted, and a dessert-spoonful of noyeau; pour this upon the preserve; put the pudding into a pretty quick oven, and bake for forty minutes.

CREAM PANCAKES.

Take half a pint of thick cream, two ounces of sugar, and a teaspoonful of finely-powdered spice; beat the yolks of three eggs, add them to the cream, mix well together; simply rub your pan with a bit of friture, make it hot, put in a small quantity of the batter, so as to have the pancakes as thin as possible. Serve them sprinkled over with grated lemon-peel and pounded loaf-sugar.

RHUBARB TART, OR SPRING PIE

Take your stalks of rhubarb, peel off the outer skin and cut them into pieces of about three inches long; pack them closely into a pie-dish lined with a rim of light paste; add a good deal of sugar, put on a top crust, and bake it for an hour in a gentle oven.

N.B.—No water should be put to a rhubarb tart, for the vegetable is of so juicy a nature that most epicures evaporate it by keeping the stalks some days before using them.

If possible, custards should be served with these tarts, their great acidity needing to be corrected by a similar addition.

PLAIN CUSTARDS.

Sweeten a pint of new milk, beat into it the yolks of four eggs and the whites of two; strain it into your cups and bake for a few minutes in a gay oven; or it may be thickened over the fire, and afterwards put into glasses as wanted. Custard made thus, from having no particular flavour, can be eaten with anything.

RAISIN PUDDING.

Mix together half a pound each of stoned raisins, chopped suet, and bread-crumbs; add four well-beaten eggs, a teacupful of milk, a little salt, and a spoonful of grated ginger. Boil it for four hours in a buttered mould or floured cloth. Pour a little brandy over it before serving.

LEMON CHEESECAKES.

Well beat and strain the yolks of six eggs and the whites of four, mix them with a quarter of a pound of very fresh butter, a pound of loaf-sugar, and the juice or grated rinds of three lemons; boil this for half an hour, stirring it constantly to prevent its burning; when done, add two ounces of grated and sifted biscuit, line your patty-pans with a puff-paste; put in the preserve, and bake them immediately.

PERSIAN PUDDING.

Take the pulp of six baked apples; add to them one ounce of rice previously boiled in milk, and beaten smooth, one ounce of sifted sugar, the grated rind of a lemon, and a teaspoonful of lemon-juice; mix these well together; then beat the whites of four eggs to a fine froth, put in the other ingredients, whisk it all up quickly, put it into a warm mould, and place it in a tolerably quick oven; when properly set, turn it out and pour round it a custard made with the yolks of the eggs remaining from the pudding.

ALMOND TARTS.

Make a very fine paste with half a pound of blanched almonds beaten in a mortar, a quarter of a pound of powdered loaf-sugar, a tablespoonful each of brandy and cream, a little nutmeg, the crumb of two stale sponge-cakes, and, if you can procure it, a little spinach-juice to colour it green. When perfectly smooth, lay it either in patty-pans, or in a tart mould lined with a light paste; bake for a quarter of an hour in a gentle oven, and before serving, decorate the top with small pieces of candied orange-chips. It may be eaten hot or cold.

PRUNE PUDDING.

Make a stiff batter with four well-beaten eggs, two ounces of sugar, a teacupful of new milk, half a pound of French prunes, six ounces of chopped veal or beef-suet, six ounces of stale bread-crumbs, and a tablespoonful of brandy. When well mixed, let it stand for two hours, then thoroughly stir it up, and boil it in a basin or a cloth for the same length of time. Serve with rich melted butter and spiced sugar.

PLAIN SUET DUMPLINGS.

Make a light paste with eight ounces of flour and four ounces of shred suet, sufficient water, a little salt, sugar, and ginger; divide this into four dumplings, put them into boiling water, and do them for half an hour. Serve with jam-sauce, sultana-sauce, or lemon-juice and sugar, apart.

TRANSPARENT PUDDING.

Put six well-beaten eggs into a saucepan with six ounces each of fresh butter and finely-pounded loaf-sugar; place it upon the fire, and stir it gently until it attains the consistency of a light batter; then let it cool. Roll a puff-paste very thin, lay it round the rim of your dish, pour in the eggs, etc., strew a little grated nutmeg on the top, and bake it for half an hour in a moderately-heated oven.

ORANGE CUSTARDS.

Boil the rind of half a Seville orange until it is perfectly tender; take it up, and beat it smooth; add to it the juice of a Seville orange, a tablespoonful of the best pale brandy, four ounces of pounded loaf-sugar, and the beaten yolks of six eggs. Whisk all well together for ten minutes, then by degrees pour in a pint of boiling milk. Keep beating until it is cold, then put the custard into cups, and place them in a shallow pan of boiling water to set. Stick some very thin pieces of candied orange chips over the tops, and serve either hot or cold.

BREAD PUDDING, BOILED.

Put a pint of new milk into a saucepan, place it upon the fire, and stir in four ounces of fresh butter: as soon as this is melted, throw in as much grated white bread as will make it pretty thick: add two ounces of sugar, a little salt, ginger, and nutmeg, four beaten eggs, and a spoonful of rose-water; when all is well mixed, put it into a buttered basin and boil it for half an hour. Serve with any sauce preferred.

Two ounces of sultana raisins or cleaned currants may be added to this pudding if approved of.

HASTY FRITTERS.

Make a light batter with half a pint of fresh mild ale and sufficient flour: add a few currants or chopped apples; beat it up briskly: have some very hot friture in a frying-pan, drop in the batter, a spoonful at a time, turn the fritters with an egg-slice, and, when browned on both sides, lay them in a dish, throw sifted loaf-sugar over them, and serve garnished with orange cut into slices and quartered.

THE BUCKINGHAM PUDDING.

Chop a pound of suet very fine, add to it half a pound of raisins stoned and halved, two eggs, a little nutmeg and ginger, two spoonfuls of flour, and the same of sugar. Mix these ingredients, together; put the pudding into a well-floured cloth, boil it for four hours, and serve with wine-sauce.

THE PRIOR'S PUDDING.

Beat half a pound of fresh butter to a cream; add two eggs, beat these also; then gradually mix in half a pound of flour, two ounces of sugar, and a little nutmeg. Put it into a small basin, tie it down, and boil it an hour and a half. No liquid is required in this pudding.

FAMILY RICE PUDDING, BAKED.

Butter a pie-dish, and put into it a quarter of a pound of rice, a tablespoonful each of chopped suet and sugar, a teaspoonful of powdered allspice, and a quart of milk. Lay it in a moderate oven, and bake it for rather more than an hour. If skim-milk be used, this is a very inexpensive dish.

PLUM PUDDING, BAKED.

Make a smooth batter with two eggs, a pint of milk, and the requisite quantity of flour; then add a pound of chopped suet, the peel of a lemon shred fine, and a pound of either raisins or currants; stir it all well together, put the pudding into a shallow well-buttered dish, and bake it for forty minutes in a pretty brisk oven. This or any other kind of plum pudding eats well when warmed up either by frying, toasting, or baking it in slices.

NEW COLLEGE PUDDING, BOILED.

Take three-quarters of a pound of fine bread-crumbs, three-quarters of a pound of suet shred small, and three-quarters of a pound of currants first washed and dried in a cloth: add a little spice, and mix with six well-beaten eggs: tie it in a floured cloth, and boil it for three hours.

POUND PUDDING.

Take half a pound of fresh butter, and an equal weight of sugar: beat the butter to a cream, then add six very well-whisked eggs, half a pound of flour, four ounces of currants, two ounces of candied lemon-peel shred fine, and a little lemon-juice. Beat all together for a quarter of an hour; put it into a buttered mould, and boil it for two hours and a half.

CHOCOLATE TART.

Well beat the yolks of six eggs, add to them two dessert-spoonsful of flour, half a pint of new milk, two ounces of sugar, the fresh-grated rind of a lemon, a teaspoonful of powdered cinnamon, and a quarter of a pound of the best French chocolate scraped smooth. Put all this into a saucepan, stir it over the fire until it gets pretty thick, then let it stand until cold. Line a tart mould with a thin puff-paste, lay in the pudding, beat up the whites of the eggs to a very high froth, put them on the top, and bake for twenty minutes. When done, sift sugar over it, and glaze it with a salamander.

MILK PANCAKES.

Put four yolks and two whites of eggs into a pint of milk, and dredge in flour until you have a smooth light batter; add a teaspoonful of grated ginger and a glass of brandy. Well heat some friture in your frying-pan, and fry your pancakes of a nice brown colour; drain them carefully from the fat, and serve with pounded and sifted sugar strewn over them. Garnish the dish with sliced lemon.

MARCH.

In this month we generally find ourselves in full Lent; but in the eyes of epicures the culinary dullness of the season is somewhat redeemed by the increased abundance of eggs, through which we are enabled upon the *jours gras* to allow ourselves many a pudding, etc., hitherto entirely beyond our reach. Our almond puddings, our amber tarts, or our egg pies can now be enjoyed in comfort, without being pained by any harrowing considerations of the expense they entail. Now, if ever, we can afford to be generous in the composition of our custards; can indulge handsomely and unhesitatingly in omelettes, and no longer be parsimonious in the preparation of our pancakes. We can likewise continue to be lavish of our lemons, extravagant of our oranges; and upon the enjoined *jours maigres* can appease our appetites, if not our consciences, by something more luxuriously lenten than dishes compounded of those pretended refreshments ycleped "bottled fruits;" for even upon Fridays delicate little *morçeaux* such as *Beignets de fruits* and fanciful fritters are permitted at our repasts, provided they are reconciled to our scruples by being fried in olive oil instead of lard or butter. But I shall not here supply you with recipes for the production of pastry allowable in Lent, as I hold the opinion that those who profess to fast should do it honestly and thoroughly, and not only be frugal in their every-day diet, but abstain from pastry altogether: still as anniversary celebrations occur at all seasons, and we are as often called upon to keep a birthday or coming of age in Lent as at any other time, it is necessary to know what cheer we can furnish upon these occasions of family festivity, and the bill of fare presented for this month is as replete with attractions as the most ardent epicure could desire.

PUDDINGS, ETC., FOR MARCH.

Almond Pudding, baked.
Custard Fritters.
Lent Minced Pie.
Amber Tart.
Egg Pie.
French Barley Pudding.
Omelette aux Confitures.
Rice Pancakes.
Date Pudding, baked.
Baked Custards.
Rolled Pudding.
Rhubarb Pudding.

Citron Cheesecakes.
Oat Pudding, baked.
Cheese-curd Puddings.
Oxford Dumplings.
Lemon Pudding.
Beignets d'Orange.
Ground Rice Pudding, baked.
Bockings.
Bread Pudding, baked.
College Puddings, fried.
Orange Pudding, baked.
Plain Boiled Rice.

ALMOND PUDDING, BAKED.

Take three ounces and a half of white bread-crumbs; steep them in a pint of new milk; then beat half a pint of blanched sweet almonds very fine till they form a paste; add the yolks of six eggs and the whites of four, a spoonful of orange-flower water, a quarter of a pound of powdered loaf-sugar, and a quarter of a pound of fresh butter, first melted; mix all well together, put it into a dish lined with a rich but thin puff-paste, and bake it for three-quarters of an hour. When eggs are cheap this is by no means an expensive pudding, and will be found excellent.

CUSTARD FRITTERS.

Beat the yolks of four eggs with a dessert-spoonful of flour, a little nutmeg, salt, and brandy; add half a pint of cream; sweeten it to taste, and bake it in a small dish for a quarter of an hour. When cold, cut it into quarters, and dip them into a batter made with a quarter of a pint each of milk and cream, the whites of the four eggs, a little flour, and a good bit of grated ginger; fry them of a nice brown; grate sugar over them, and serve them as hot as possible.

LENT MINCED PIE.

Take the yolks and whites of four hard-boiled eggs; shred them fine; add to them three or four apples pared, cored, and chopped small, half-a-pound each of dried currants and raisins stoned and cut up, two ounces of sugar, a quarter of a pound of mixed candied-peel, and the juice of two Seville oranges. Stir the whole well together; line a dish with a puff-paste, lay in your mince, cover it with a top crust, and bake for three-quarters of an hour in a gentle oven. If preferred, you can make it into small pies, and bake them for twenty minutes.

AMBER TART.

Beat a quarter of a pound of fresh candied orange-peel until it is a paste; put it into a saucepan in which you have melted a pound of very fresh butter; add three-quarters of a pound of finely-powdered loaf-sugar; stir all together, then put in the well-beaten yolks of twelve eggs. When sufficiently thick, pour it into a tart-mould lined with a light paste; put a cover of crust over it, and bake it in a slow oven for forty minutes; when done, lift it out of the dish, and serve it either hot or cold.

EGG PIE.

Take a pound of either marrow or fine beef-suet chopped small, twelve eggs boiled hard and minced, a little beaten cinnamon and grated nutmeg, a pound of currants, washed, picked, and dried in a cloth, two or three spoonsful of cream or new milk to moisten it, a quarter of a pound of powdered loaf-sugar, and a glass of brandy. Mix it well together, and put it into a dish lined with a puff-paste, bake it for an hour or forty minutes, according to the heat of your oven, and, when done, squeeze in the juice of a lemon, and pour a little cream upon the top. This is best if eaten hot.

FRENCH BARLEY PUDDING.

Boil half a pound of the best French barley in milk, until the barley is quite soft, then stir in half a pound of fresh butter, a quarter of a pound of loaf-sugar, and four yolks and two whites of eggs well beaten; add a little rose or orange-flower water, and put it into a well-buttered pie-dish. Bake it for an hour.

OMELETTE AUX CONFITURES.

Well beat six or eight eggs, add a dessert-spoonful of milk or brandy, to prevent the omelette from being hard; sweeten it to taste; heat some friture in a pan over the fire, pour in your eggs, and when well set and brown on the under side, it is done, omelettes not requiring to be turned in the pan. Have ready some marmalade, jam, or currant-jelly, previously melted by warming it in the oven or on the hob, spread it upon the upper side of the omelette, fold it double, pour more preserve over it, and strew sugar on the top.

RICE PANCAKES.

Take a quarter of a pound of ground rice, put it into rather more than a pint of milk, and keep stirring it until it is as thick as pap; then put in a a quarter of a pound of butter and half a grated nutmeg. Pour it into a pan, and when quite cold, stir in four eggs well beaten, two spoonsful of powdered white sugar, and enough flour to make it of the consistency of batter. Mix the whole well together, and fry portions of it as pancakes over a quick fire.

DATE PUDDING, BAKED.

Take half a pound of fine Tafilat dates, stone them, and pound them to a paste; add the juice of a lemon, a quarter of a pound of fresh butter, the beaten yolks of six eggs, a gill of brandy, four ounces of powdered and sifted loaf-sugar and two ounces of stale bread-crumbs. Thoroughly mix all together, put it into a buttered mould, and bake for twenty minutes in a moderate oven.

BAKED CUSTARDS.

Boil some mace and cinnamon in a pint of cream and let the cream grow cold; then take four yolks and two whites of eggs beaten and strained, a little rose or laurel water, and nutmeg and sugar to your taste. Mix them well together, and bake for about five or seven minutes in small custard-cups.

ROLLED PUDDING.

Mix six ounces of shred beef-suet with ten ounces of flour and enough water to make it into a light paste; roll it out flat, but not too thin, and spread upon the surface either jam or marmalade, treacle or honey, or sprinkle it thickly over with dried currants, chopped apple, or raisins stoned and cut up small; make it into a roll; fasten the ends together, tie it in a cloth, and well boil it. When served, cut it into five or six pieces, and pour melted butter over it. Instead of being boiled, it may be baked for an hour, and served with sugar strewn over it.

RHUBARB PUDDING.

Make a good suet-paste; line your pudding-basin; cut your rhubarb into short lengths about the size of gooseberries; add the rind of a lemon pared as thin as possible, a good slice of butter, and plenty of sugar. A few chopped almonds are likewise a considerable improvement. Pack in the rhubarb as tightly as you can, but do not add any water: cover it with a top crust, tie a floured cloth over it, and boil for an hour or more, according to the size of the pudding.

It is almost unnecessary to say that puddings of every description should be put into boiling water, which should never be suffered to go off the boil, otherwise the pudding will be heavy.

CITRON CHEESECAKES.

Gradually mix the beaten yolks of four eggs with a quart of boiled cream; when it is become quite cold, set it on the fire again, and let it boil until it turns to curds. Take two ounces each of blanched almonds, sweet biscuits, and candied citron-peel; pound these in a mortar, moistening them with a little lemon-juice. Mix the curds with them, sweeten it to your palate, and when cold, put it into patty-pans lined with a very light crust. Bake for about ten minutes.

OAT PUDDING, BAKED.

Swell one pound of whole groats by putting them over night to soak in a quart of new milk: add a quarter of a pound each of currants washed and picked, raisins stoned, and half a pound of veal-suet finely shred, four well-beaten eggs, and sugar to the taste; add plenty of ginger, mix the whole thoroughly together, and bake in a well-buttered mould for an hour and a half.

CHEESE-CURD PUDDINGS.

Turn a gallon of milk with rennet; drain off the whey; put the curd into a mortar with six ounces of fresh butter; beat it till the curd and butter are well incorporated; then whisk the yolks of six eggs and the whites of three; strain them into the curd, and add three pounded macaroons. Mix all together, and sweeten to your taste. Butter your patty-pans and fill them: bake in a moderate oven for seven or ten minutes. When done, turn them into a dish: cut candied orange-peel into short lengths, and some blanched almonds into long slips; stick them about the puddings; pour melted butter into the dish, and throw some sifted sugar over all.

OXFORD DUMPLINGS.

Take finely-shred beef-suet and currants, of each eight ounces, the crumbs of grated bread four ounces, four dessert-spoonsful of flour, the thinly-shred rind of a lemon, two ounces of sugar, some allspice and ginger, four eggs, and a sufficiency of milk to make it moist enough. Mix well, and make it into twelve dumplings, and fry them in plenty of friture until they are of a nice brown colour. Serve them with sweet sauce.

LEMON PUDDING.

Add the juice of two lemons and the grated rind of one, to eight eggs well beaten; then melt six ounces of butter, pour it over six ounces of powdered loaf-sugar, and stir it one way until it is quite cold; put it with the eggs and lemon, mix it well together, and lay it in a tart-dish edged with paste: bake it for half an hour.

BEIGNETS D'ORANGE.

Beignets are a neat little dish, something similar to fritters, only that the fruit employed in the composition of beignets, instead of being minced or sliced thin, is cut into rather thick pieces and soaked in warm brandy before being dipped into batter. Beignets d'orange are made thus: carefully tear off the peel, and with a sharp knife cut the oranges into tolerably thick slices; take away the pips, and lay the fruit to soak in brandy placed in a saucepan upon the hob. Then prepare a batter by mixing enough flour with half a pint of milk to form a light batter; add the white of an egg beaten to a froth, and a dessert-spoonful of brandy. Drain your slices of fruit, dip them into the batter, and fry them quickly in some boiling friture. Serve with sifted sugar plentifully strewn over them in the dish.

GROUND RICE PUDDING, BAKED.

Boil a quarter of a pound of ground rice in a quart of new milk with a few chips of cinnamon. Stir it frequently to prevent its sticking to the saucepan. When it is pretty thick, pour it into a pan, stir in a quarter of a pound of fresh butter, sugar to your taste, half a grated nutmeg, and a little rose or orange-flower water; stir it well together, and let it grow cold; then beat six eggs, mix them with the rice, put it into a buttered dish, and bake it for forty minutes. You may line the rim of the dish with an edging of paste or not, according to fancy.

BOCKINGS.

Mix four ounces of buck-wheat flour with a breakfast-cupful of lukewarm milk; place it before the fire to rise, and in about an hour add to it six well-beaten eggs and a sufficiency of milk to form it into a smooth batter. Fry portions at a time as you would for pancakes, and serve sprinkled with powdered loaf-sugar.

BREAD PUDDING, BAKED.

Crumble up a penny-roll; take an equal weight of flour, the yolks of four and the whites of two eggs, two teaspoonsful of ginger, half a pound of raisins, stoned, half a pound of currants washed clean and dried, and four ounces of sugar. Mix it all together, and then stir in as much hot milk as will make it into a good batter. Butter a pie-dish, put in the pudding, lay a few bits of butter on the top, and bake it for an hour.

COLLEGE PUDDINGS, FRIED.

Pound and sift a quarter of a pound of hard biscuit, add to it a quarter of a pound of suet finely chopped, half a pound of currants washed and dried, a little sugar, nutmeg, and salt, and three eggs, with as much milk or cream as will make a stiff batter. Put a spoonful at a time into a frying-pan of hot lard, and when done, serve the puddings garnished with chips of candied lemon-peel.

ORANGE PUDDING, BAKED.

Grate off the outer rind of two large Seville oranges; put the oranges into plenty of water, and boil them till tender; then open them, free them from the pips, and beat them in a mortar until they are a smooth paste; add half a pound of white sugar, the grated orange-peel, four dessert-spoonsful of thick cream, the yolks of six eggs, well beaten, a tablespoonful of brandy, and a quarter of a pound of butter, melted. Line a small tart-mould with a light paste; lay in your pudding, and bake it for forty minutes.

PLAIN BOILED RICE.

Take a quarter of a pound of rice and half a pound of sultana raisins; tie them in a cloth, allowing the rice room to swell. Boil it two hours; turn it out, and pour over it melted butter, sugar, and nutmeg. Or it may be boiled without the raisins, and serve jam-sauce or currant-sauce apart.

APRIL.

———

SPRING is coming to us once again; already the verdant fields rejoice our sight, and enrich the quality of the milk, cream, and butter which lend perfection to those puddings that we presently enjoy, while the blooming fruit-trees give gracious promise of many a pleasant pudding for us *in prospectu*. And not alone upon horticultural assistance do we need depend; the hedge-row flowers and garden vegetables will likewise contribute to extend our resources for stimulating and gratifying our epicurean predilections; for notwithstanding it may appear to some a downright heresy for us to pervert the blossoms of the earth to culinary uses, and it may be imagined that one must be hard pushed for a pudding when reduced to descend to the vegetable creation for the requisite materials, yet from its vernal prestige there is really quite a sentiment attached to cowslip pudding; and as to tansy fritters and spinach tarts, they may successfully compete with any preparation the art of cookery has ever produced.

PUDDINGS, ETC., FOR APRIL.

Chestnut Pudding, baked.
Cabinet Pudding.
Batter Pudding, boiled.
Rice Cheesecakes.
Lemon Custards.
Cowslip Pudding.
Royal Fritters.
Marrow Pudding.
Yeast Dumplings.
Curd Puffs.
Omelette au Sucre.
Saffron Pudding, for Easter.

Lemon Tarts.
Boiled Rice Pudding.
Almond Cheesecakes.
Beignets de Patisserie.
Bread Dumplings.
Italian Pudding.
Orange Tartlets.
College Puddings, baked.
Inexpensive Lemon Pudding.
French Flummery.
Adelaide Pudding.
Shelford Pudding.

CHESTNUT PUDDING, BAKED.

Boil twelve large chestnuts for a quarter of an hour, then peel and beat them in a mortar, with a little white wine, till they form a fine paste; add the beaten yolks of six eggs and the whites of two, a quarter of a pound of butter, melted, and half a pint of cream, or the same quantity of milk previously boiled down to a custard. Mix all together, sweeten to your taste, put it into a saucepan and stir it over the fire till it thickens, then lay it in a dish lined with a rich puff-paste, and bake for forty minutes.

CABINET PUDDING.

Take eight sponge cakes, four ounces of sultana raisins soaked in brandy, and the yolks of four eggs, and the whites of three. Butter a mould; stick the raisins about it to form a pattern; break the sponge-cakes into convenient pieces, and with them line the mould; then make a custard with the eggs, adding sugar and nutmeg to taste; pour it into the mould; tie a cloth over it, and put it into a large pot, about one-third full of boiling water. Boil it gently for half an hour; when done, turn it out, and serve with brandy sauce.

BATTER PUDDING, BOILED.

Beat and strain four eggs upon four spoonsful of flour; mix well, and gradually dilute it with a pint of new milk; add a good teaspoonful of ginger and a little salt: tie it in a floured cloth, or put it into a buttered basin, and boil it one hour. Serve with melted butter, lemon, and sugar.

RICE CHEESECAKES.

Take four ounces of rice, ground or whole, according to fancy, and boil it in milk till it is quite done; then put in half a pound of butter, half a pint of cream, six ounces of loaf-sugar pounded and sifted, a glass of brandy, and four eggs well beaten. Mix all well together, and put it into raised crusts, and bake them for a quarter of an hour. Observe, all cheese-cakes should be put into the oven as soon as they are made, otherwise they turn oily.

LEMON CUSTARDS.

Beat the whites and yolks of four eggs; strain them, and add two large tablespoonsful of lemon-juice, four ounces of powdered loaf-sugar, the grated rind of one lemon, and a glass each of white wine and brandy. Mix all well together, and stir it in a small saucepan over the fire until it becomes sufficiently thick; then pour it into small cups, and serve.

COWSLIP PUDDING.

Pull some cowslips from their stems until you have a quart of flowers; bruise them, boil them in a pint of milk or cream, and when they begin to get tender, pour them into a dish, and add to them four well-beaten eggs, a quarter of a pound of Naples biscuit, or bread-crumbs grated and soaked in milk, and a good piece of butter: mix it all together; put it into a buttered dish, and bake it for an hour. When done, pour a rich wine sauce over it, and serve.

ROYAL FRITTERS.

Boil a quart of new milk, and pour in a pint of white wine: take it off the fire, let it stand five minutes, skim off the curd, and beat it up well with six eggs and a little nutmeg. Add flour sufficient to make it the proper consistency of batter, put in some sugar, and fry the fritters over a quick fire.

MARROW PUDDING.

Grate six ounces of biscuits, shred six ounces of beef-marrow, stone four ounces of raisins, and add candied orange or lemon peel and sugar, of each two ounces, with nutmeg to the taste. Line a pie-dish with a rich crust, lay in the ingredients, and beat up four eggs in half a pint of new milk or cream; pour this over the pudding, and bake it for one hour and a half in a gentle oven. Sift powdered loaf-sugar over it before serving.

YEAST DUMPLINGS.

Of flour, milk, and yeast make a light dough, in the same manner as you would bread; place it before the fire to rise, and, when it is become pretty light, make it into small dumplings of about the size of hens' eggs; throw them into boiling water; see that they float properly; boil them for twenty minutes. Take them up, stick them over with bits of candied peel, and serve them with a lemon or ginger sauce apart.

CURD PUFFS.

Curd a quart of new milk, strain it from the whey, then rub the curd through a hair-sieve, and add to it four ounces of bread-crumbs, two ounces of fresh butter, half a glass of wine, the grated rind of a lemon, and sugar to your taste. Rub small cups with butter, lay in your puffs, and let them remain for thirty minutes in a very cool oven.

OMELETTE AU SUCRE.

Take eight eggs, beat them well, add an ounce of fine loaf-sugar, and fry it quickly over a bright fire. Then place it in a dish, strew sugar over it, glaze it with a salamander, and serve hot.

SAFFRON PUDDING, FOR EASTER.

Take a pound of bread-crumbs, soak them in a strong infusion of saffron, which should have been prepared beforehand; then beat the yolks of six eggs and the whites of four until they are very highly frothed; add to them a quarter of a pound of candied citron-peel cut into lozenge-shaped pieces of about an inch long, a quarter of a pound of blanched almonds halved, a pound of the suet from a fat loin of veal, chopped lightly, and a gill of brandy; mix bread-crumbs, etc., together; put it into a buttered dish, and bake it for an hour and a half. Beef-suet may be used when veal-suet cannot be procured, but the latter, on account of its greater delicacy, is much to be preferred.

LEMON TARTS.

Mix well together the juice and grated rinds of two large lemons, half a pound of powdered loaf-sugar, two eggs, and the crumb of two sponge-cakes: beat it thoroughly smooth, and put it into twelve patty-pans, lined with a light puff-paste: bake them until the crust is done.

A BOILED RICE PUDDING.

Swell six ounces of whole rice by scalding it in a quart of new milk; let it grow cold, then mix it with a quarter of a pound of currants well washed and rubbed dry, a quarter of a pound of white sugar, and two eggs well beaten. Mix the whole well together; put it into a buttered basin or floured cloth, and boil for forty minutes. Serve it with any sauce you like.

ALMOND CHEESECAKES.

Take four ounces of blanched almonds, beat them in a mortar with two spoonsful of rose-water, then add the yolks of four eggs well whisked, and four ounces of pounded and sifted white sugar. Work it well until it froths, then put it into patty-pans lined with a fine puff-paste. Bake for about twenty minutes in a moderate oven.

BEIGNETS DE PATISSERIE.

In making pastry there is often a small quantity over and above what is required: this should be rolled thin, cut into narrow strips or stamped into any form agreeable, and dipped into a little brandy, white sugar, and egg, and fried brown. Serve with sugar dusted over them. Small slices of cold paste or stale cake are likewise very good if dressed in the above manner, but the latter should be soaked some time before frying.

BREAD DUMPLINGS.

Melt two ounces of butter in a breakfast-cupful of hot new milk, and add enough sifted bread-crumbs to make it a very stiff paste: let it stand till cold, then stir in two eggs, a teaspoonful of ginger, two ounces of candied orange or lemon peel cut into little square pieces not much larger than currants, or the latter may be used instead. Work it well together, form it into dumplings, and either bake them in a dish or boil them in a cloth for twenty minutes.

ITALIAN PUDDING.

Boil four bruised bay-leaves in a pint of new milk; at the end of five minutes remove them, and gradually pour the milk upon two ounces of potato-flour, previously rubbed very smooth in a good drop of cream. Let it grow cold, then take six eggs, break them, and carefully separate the yolks and whites, the former being kept whole, and put one at a time into boiling water, then, when done hard, cut into large sized dice. Beat up the whites to a froth; add a little cream and white sugar to taste: put this to the milk, etc., and then gently stir in the pieces of yolk. Line a tart-dish with a very rich crust; lay in your pudding; put a little butter or olive oil on the top, and bake for forty minutes.

I first tasted this dish in Tuscany on the 27th April, 1850, and I have commemorated the event by having a like pudding annually on that day ever since.

ORANGE TARTLETS.

Line your patty-pans with a very rich puff-paste; put a small quantity of orange marmalade into each, and squeeze fresh Seville orange juice plentifully upon them: bake for a quarter of an hour or twenty minutes. Sift pounded sugar over them, and serve either hot or cold.

COLLEGE PUDDINGS, BAKED.

Take half a pint of good new milk or cream, put it into a saucepan, and let it come to a boil, then take it off the fire and stir in half a pound of butter: let it get cold, and add to it the yolks of eight well-beaten eggs and the whites of four, two ounces of loaf-sugar pounded and sifted, and a quarter of a pound of flour first moistened with a little of the cold milk. Mix all well together, let it stand for half an hour in a warm place: put it into a buttered dish and bake it for forty minutes in a pretty quick oven.

INEXPENSIVE LEMON PUDDING.

Grate the rinds of two lemons, rubbing the grater well with a quarter of a pound of sifted loaf-sugar, add a quarter of a pound of finely-shred beef-suet, four eggs well whisked, the juice of a lemon, and a tablespoonful of white wine; work the ingredients well together, put them into a buttered basin, tie it well down and boil for forty minutes. Serve with plain melted butter and sugar.

FRENCH FLUMMERY.

Put half an ounce of the best isinglass into a quart of cream or good new milk. Let it simmer gently over a slow fire for twenty minutes; then take it off, sweeten it to your taste, and put in a spoonful each of rose and orange-flower water: strain it into a mould, and when quite cold, turn it out upon a dish. Garnish it round with fruits preserved whole in syrup.

ADELAIDE PUDDING.

Take the yolks of seven eggs and the whites of four; dissolve ten ounces of loaf-sugar in a pint of warm water, add to it the eggs, whisk them for nearly half an hour, gradually dredge in a pound of flour, flavour with the juice and grated rind of a lemon; pour it into a mould, and place it immediately in a pretty hot oven for an hour.

SHELFORD PUDDING.

Well beat six eggs, and add them to one pound of suet, one pound of flour, three-quarters of a pound of currants, carefully cleaned, a little salt, some sugar, grated lemon-peel, and a teacupful of milk. Mix it well and boil it in a pudding-shape for six hours. Serve with wine or brandy sauce.

MAY.

OUR appetites at this time appear to increase with the brightening days, and since game no longer plays its important part at our entertainments, we are more than ever inclined to console ourselves with the sweet solace of pastry: at the same time I am obliged to admit that we no longer willingly content ourselves with the winter fare that dried fruits helped us to furnish, but, with the avidity of birds, levy contributions upon our currant, gooseberry, apricot, and also upon our cherry trees, justifying our greediness for "green puddings" with the excuse that the after-fruit comes all the finer from early judicious thinnings, and that the flavour of that we now enjoy is the more preferable when it "tastes of the wood:" the last idea, however, is an entire delusion; nothing is more desirable than maturity in all things, and more especially in fruit. Nevertheless, May is proverbially the month for merry-makings, and Whitsuntide the customary period to begin our gooseberry puddings, so let us rejoice and be glad in everything May gives us—even its green currants, its tansy leaves, and its chilly days, that the genial joys of the table do quite as much to enliven as its coyly-opening flowers and its inconstant skies.

PUDDINGS, ETC., FOR MAY.

Conservative Pudding.
Nonpareil Pudding.
Vine-leaf Fritters.
Green Apricot Tart.
Spinach Pudding.
Bread Cheesecakes.
Old-fashioned Gooseberry
  Pudding.
Norfolk Dumplings.
Omelette Soufflée.
Green Currant Pudding.
Almond Custards.
Tart de Moi.

Vermicelli Pudding, boiled.
Curd Cheesecakes.
Small Biscuit Puddings.
Sago Pudding.
Calves' Feet Pie.
Green Currant Tart.
Almond Fraze.
Tansy Fritters.
Sweetmeat Pudding.
Blanc Manger.
Montagu Pudding.
League Pudding.

CONSERVATIVE PUDDING.

Soak two ounces each of macaroons, ratafia, and sponge-cakes, in half a pint of cream; then beat them well, and add to them the whisked yolks of eight eggs, and a tablespoonful of brandy. Butter a deep mould, arrange in it some sultana raisins or dried cherries; pour in the pudding, cover it with a cloth, lay it in a stew-pan containing a little boiling water, and simmer it for an hour and forty minutes. Be careful that the water does not reach the pudding. When done, turn it into a dish, and serve with brandy sauce.

NONPAREIL PUDDING.

Take half a pound each of flour, suet, treacle, and raisins, stoned and halved; one egg, one tablespoonful of milk, and a little grated lemon-peel; put it into a buttered mould, and boil it two hours. Serve with egg or spice sauce.

VINE-LEAF FRITTERS.

Gather some of the smallest vine leaves you can get; cut off the stalks, and lay them to soak in a little French brandy, rasped lemon-peel, and sugar. Then make a batter with flour, water, and the white of egg; drop a small portion here and there over the pan, lay a vine-leaf upon each, fry them very quick, and when done, strew sugar over them. Glaze them with a salamander, and serve with lemon-juice and sugar.

GREEN APRICOT TART.

Take your young green apricots before the stone is formed, lay them in a saucepan with plenty of sugar and water; simmer them gently until perfectly tender, then take them up, reduce the syrup in which they were boiled, put them into a tart-dish lined with a rim of puff-paste, pour in the liquor, cover them with a top crust, and bake for forty minutes in a moderate oven.

SPINACH PUDDING.

Take half a gallon of spinach very well washed and picked; put it into a saucepan with a teaspoonful of salt; when it is tender enough, turn it into a sieve to drain. Then chop it up fine, and mix it well with a quarter of a pound of butter, melted, a little nutmeg, a quarter of a pound of sugar, half a pint of cream, the yolks of six eggs and the whites of four, and a quarter of a pound of fine breadcrumbs: mix all well together; put it into a saucepan again, and continue stirring it until it thickens. Then wet and flour your cloth, tie your pudding in it, put it into boiling water, and let it boil an hour. When done, turn it into a dish, pour melted butter over it, and add the juice of a Seville orange. If preferred, you can put it into a tart-dish edged with a rim of crust, and bake it.

BREAD CHEESECAKES.

Slice a stale halfpenny-roll as thin as possible; pour upon it half a pint of scalding hot cream, and let it stand two hours to soak. Then take four eggs, a quarter of a pound of butter, and half a nutmeg, grated. Beat all well together; put in a quarter of a pound of currants, washed and dried before the fire, and a dessert-spoonful of brandy. Bake in patty-pans or in raised crusts for twenty minutes.

OLD-FASHIONED GOOSEBERRY PUDDING.

Nicely pick the stems and tops from the gooseberries; wash them, and put them into a good-sized pudding-basin lined with a tolerably thick suet-crust, add two tablespoonsful of sugar, but no *water* or *spices*; cover it with a crust, tie a floured cloth over it, and boil for two hours in plenty of boiling water. Turn it into a dish when done; and at table stir in two ounces of butter, and add more sugar before serving.

NORFOLK DUMPLINGS.

Take two eggs, a little salt, and half a pint of new milk, mix this into rather a stiff batter with a sufficiency of flour. Have ready a saucepan of boiling water, and drop your batter into it a spoonful at a time. In two or three minutes the dumplings will be done. Throw them into a sieve to drain, then lay them in your dish, and stir a lump of fresh butter among them. Serve as hot as possible. Fruit sauce may be had with them if preferred.

OMELETTE SOUFFLÉE.

Carefully break eight eggs, separate the whites from the yolks, beat the whites to a snow, mix the yolks with a little grated lemon-peel and a spoonful of sugar; then mix the whites and yolks together, put them into a buttered dish, sprinkle it over with sugar; put the omelette into a gentle oven, and immediately it is well risen, serve it dusted over with sifted sugar.

GREEN CURRANT PUDDING.

Take the currants as soon as they are large enough, pick them from their stalks, put them into a pudding-basin lined with a light suet-crust, add plenty of sugar, cover them with a paste, and, if it is a pint pudding, boil it for two hours; a larger size requires to be boiled longer. Serve as you would a gooseberry pudding. Many epicures prefer currants before they are ripe on account of the greater softness of the pips, which, when eaten old, are very disagreeable.

ALMOND CUSTARDS.

Beat a quarter of a pound of blanched sweet almonds until they are a very smooth paste; add to them a pint of cream, two spoonsful each of rose-water and powdered loaf-sugar, and the well-beaten yolks of four eggs. Put it into a saucepan over the fire; stir it one way till it is sufficiently thick, then put it into your cups.

TART DE MOI.

Line a tart-mould with a rim of light puff-paste, then fill it with alternate layers of grated biscuit or macaroons, shred marrow or veal suet, and different kinds of sweetmeats until your dish is sufficiently filled. Then boil a quart of new milk, a lump of butter, a tablespoonful of sugar, and a dessert-spoonful of rose-water; thicken it with four well-beaten eggs, pour it into your pie-dish, and bake for an hour.

VERMICELLI PUDDING, BOILED.

Take four ounces of Italian vermicelli; crush it a little, but do not break it too small; put it into a saucepan of boiling milk, with two ounces of sweet almonds blanched and halved; retire it a little from the fire, and, when it has absorbed the milk, mix it with four ounces of fresh butter, a gill of eau-de-vie, a quarter of a pound of powdered white sugar, and the yolks of six eggs well beaten. Put it into a buttered basin, tie it down with a floured cloth, and boil it for an hour and a half. Serve with melted butter and any sauce suitable.

CURD CHEESECAKES.

Well beat four eggs; add half a pint of good curds, two table-spoonsful of rich cream, half a grated nutmeg, and a spoonful of orange-flower water; when well mixed, put in a quarter of a pound each of sugar and currants well washed and dried in a cloth. Work the whole together, line your patty-pans with a good crust, put in the mixture, and bake for twenty minutes.

SMALL BISCUIT PUDDINGS.

Take a quarter of a pint of new milk, a quarter of a pound each of grated biscuits, butter, and brown sugar, with the beaten yolks of four eggs and the whites of two; mix all well together, and bake in small cups for twenty minutes. Turn them into a dish to serve.

SAGO PUDDING, BOILED.

Boil two ounces of sago in a pint of new milk till perfectly tender; when cold, add five eggs, two ounces of bread-crumbs, a little brandy, and sugar to the taste. Mix all well together; boil it for one hour in a basin tightly covered with a floured cloth, and serve with melted butter, white wine, and sugar.

CALVES'-FEET PIE.

Put a pair of calves' feet into a saucepan with three quarts of water, and two or three blades of mace; let them boil slowly until the liquor is reduced to one-third of its original quantity. Take out the feet, pick the flesh from the bones, and lay a portion of it in a pie-dish lined with puff-paste; have half a pound each of stoned raisins and washed currants, strew them in with the remainder of the meat; put in half a pint of white wine, skim and sweeten the liquor, pour it over, cover with a top crust, and bake it for an hour and forty minutes in a moderate oven.

GREEN CURRANT TART.

Carefully pick over and stem a pint of green currants; put them into a saucepan with very little water, and just scald them; then strain them from the water, mash them up with six ounces of white sugar, three ounces of fresh butter beaten to a cream with the whites of two eggs, and a teacupful of red-currant jelly. Put a rim of very light paste round the edge of your tart-dish, lay in your fruit, and bake for half an hour.

ALMOND FRAZE.

Steep half a pound of blanched sweet almonds in half a pint of new milk or cream; after a few hours, take them out and pound them in a mortar; mix them in the milk again, and add the yolks of six eggs and the whites of four, sufficient loaf-sugar to sweeten it, and two ounces of grated bread. Stir all well together, put it into a frying-pan in which there is plenty of boiling butter, and fry it until it is tolerably well set, then lay it in a dish and strew sugar over it.

TANSY FRITTERS.

Grate the crumb of a penny-roll, and pour upon it a pint of boiling milk; when cold, add a large spoonful of brandy, the grated rind of half a lemon, sugar to taste, the yolks of four eggs well beaten, and just enough spinach and tansy juice to tinge it green. Mix this over the fire in a saucepan with a quarter of a pound of butter till pretty thick; let it stand for two hours, and then drop a spoonful at a time into boiling friture. When the fritters are done, serve with spiced sugar apart.

SWEETMEAT PUDDING.

Take a small tart-dish, line it with a thin puff-paste; slice one ounce each of candied lemon, orange, and citron peel; lay them in the dish and pour over them the beaten yolks of six eggs and the whites of three, a quarter of a pound of sugar, six ounces of fresh butter melted, and the juice of two sweet oranges. Bake it in a moderately-heated oven for half an hour.

BLANC MANGER.

Although blanc manger is not accounted so fashionable as it was formerly, yet it is so useful an entremets, that I think its insertion is here necessary.

Beat two ounces of blanched sweet almonds and six bitter almonds until they are quite a paste, mix them into a quart of rich new milk, with a quarter of an ounce of washed isinglass; boil it until the isinglass is perfectly dissolved, sweeten it to your taste, keep stirring until it is almost cold, then put it into your mould, and when nicely set, turn it into a dish and serve.

MONTAGU PUDDING.

Lightly shred half a pound of suet, add to it four tablespoonsful of flour, four tablespoonsful of milk, four eggs, half a pound of stoned raisins, and spice and sugar to taste. Well mix, and boil it in a buttered basin for four hours.

LEAGUE PUDDING.

Take one ounce of almonds blanched and halved, one ounce of raisins unstoned, and one ounce of candied orange-peel cut into rather large pieces, a dessert-spoonful of ginger, a tablespoonful of sugar, half a pound of chopped suet, and half a pound of grated and sifted bread. Mix it well together with enough milk to make it very stiff; then add four beaten eggs, put it into a floured cloth and boil for two hours.

JUNE.

Of oranges and lemons, and preserves and grocers' fruit, we are now almost independent, for the currants are beginning to turn red, and the raspberries are ripening, and the good old gooseberries are full grown, and if we call anything in aid besides our own fresh fruits, it is merely for the sake of presenting a variety; and cheesecakes and custards are never to be despised, especially when set off by a cherry tart or gooseberry pie. Some epicures too are averse to acids; and although a raspberry pudding or a gooseberry fool may be pronounced ambrosia by some, there are others who assert them to be the most objectionable edibles ever introduced. This proves that all our prejudices should be consulted by the considerate caterer; and it is gratifying to know that our gardens and larders are at this time so replete, and the resources of cookery so diversified and unlimited, that, by paying attention to the differences of taste, every one may be pleased with the provisions set before him.

PUDDINGS, ETC., FOR JUNE.

Quaking Pudding.

Gooseberry Tart.

Tansy Pudding.

Cherry Pie.

Spinach Tarts.

Gooseberry Pudding, baked.

Strawberry Tart.

Red-currant Pudding.

Lemon-peel Cheesecakes.

Custard Pudding, baked.

Pain Perdu.

Rice Balls.

Cheap Bread Pudding.

Gooseberry Fool.

Raspberry Fritters.

Plain Baked Pudding.

Frangipanni Tart.

Rice Custards.

Almond Pudding, boiled.

Omelette au Citron.

Cherry Pudding.

Reform Club Pudding.

French Prune Pudding.

Puddings in haste.

———

QUAKING PUDDING.

Well beat eight eggs, add to them the grated crumbs of a stale penny-roll, two spoonsful of ground rice, a little nutmeg and orange-flower water. Mix it smoothly together with a quart of new milk. Put it into a floured cloth, tie it rather loose, plunge it into boiling water, and boil it briskly for one hour. Serve with red or white wine sauce.

GOOSEBERRY TART.

Pick and nicely wash your gooseberries, and if possible, only use the rough or hairy sort; line the rim of a tart-dish with a very light crust, lay in the fruit, strew in a good deal of sugar, put on a top crust, and place it in a gentle oven. At the end of an hour it will be done; but if you do not intend the tart to be eaten immediately, you can open the oven-door and let it remain in the oven until it is quite cold, by this means, if the gooseberries are the right sort, they will turn red.

TANSY PUDDING.

Grate four Naples biscuits, and pour as much boiling-hot new milk over them as they will absorb. Then beat the yolks of four eggs, and chop a few tansy leaves with enough spinach-juice to make it slightly green. When the biscuits are cold, mix all together; add sufficient sugar, and set it over a slow fire to thicken; then take it off; let it grow cold, and put it into a cloth wetted and well floured; tie it up close, and boil it for forty minutes. Take it out of the water; let it stand ten minutes in a basin, then carefully turn it into a dish, and pour white sauce over it.

CHERRY PIE.

Cherry pie proper has, from time immemorial, been made in a *round* dish: the reason of this is unknown, but a cherry pie of an oval form would be an incongruity only equalled by making the table of King Arthur a square one.

If you are not provided with an earthenware dish of the requisite shape, you can get one made of tin: these I have seen used at the tables of the most refined gourmets of the day.

Take then a round dish, edge it with a rim of crust, lay a good deal of sugar at the bottom, stem your fruit, put it in, add more sugar on the top, cover it with a top crust, and bake it in a slow oven for an hour and a half.

SPINACH TARTS.

Put a sufficiency of spinach leaves for a few minutes in boiling water, then drain them dry, chop them with some butter, sugar, cream, orange-flower water, and finely shred candied citron-peel; put it into patty-pans lined with a fine puff-paste, and bake for half an hour in a gentle oven. Although only a vegetable composition, these tarts, when well made, are both delicious and salutary.

GOOSEBERRY PUDDING, BAKED.

Scald a quart of gooseberries in water until they are soft, drain them, and when cold, work them smooth with a spoon. Then add half a pound of powdered loaf-sugar, half a pound of fresh butter, four ounces of bread-crumbs, and the yolks of six and the whites of four eggs. Beat all together for a quarter of an hour: put into a buttered dish without crust, and bake it for half an hour. Strew sifted sugar over it, and serve either hot or cold.

STRAWBERRY TART.

Take the unripe or inferior fruit that you have discarded from your dessert strawberries; line a tart-dish with a rim of very rich paste, stem your fruit, and lay it in; strew some white sugar on the top, and pour in a glass of red wine; bake it for forty minutes in a gentle oven. When done, if it is to be eaten hot, pour over it some warmed cream; when eaten cold, pour some raw cream upon it before serving.

RED-CURRANT PUDDING.

Line your pudding-basin with a good crust; stem your fruit; strew sugar amongst it as you fill your basin; add more sugar on the top, cover it with a lid of paste, and boil for two hours.

LEMON-PEEL CHEESECAKES.

Boil the peel of two large lemons till it is very tender, pound it in a mortar, add a quarter of a pound of powdered loaf-sugar, half a pound of fresh butter, the beaten yolks of six eggs, and a little curd pressed fine. Pound and mix all well together; lay a puff-paste in your patty-pans, half fill them with the cheesecake, and bake them for half an hour.

CUSTARD PUDDING, BAKED.

Bruise four peach-leaves and boil them in a pint of new milk; then beat and strain the yolks of six eggs and the whites of four; add a little cream to them, and two ounces of white sugar in powder; strain the hot milk from the peach-leaves, mix it gradually with the eggs, stir it over the fire until it thickens, then put it into a buttered dish; pour a little more cream upon the top, and bake it for half an hour.

PAIN PERDU.

Cut the crust from two stale French-rolls, slice them; have ready some eggs, cream, rose-water, and sugar, all beat up together; put your bread to soak in it. Fry some lard or butter; take your slices of roll and gently lay them in the pan; do them quickly, drain them, range them neatly in a dish, strew sugar over them, and serve with spiced sugar apart.

RICE BALLS.

Boil a quarter of a pound of whole rice in rather more than a pint of new milk, add a sufficiency of white sugar, cinnamon, and a little grated lemon-peel; when the rice is quite tender, pour it out, and let it grow cold; then form it into small balls. Roll them in fine bread-crumbs and beaten egg, fry them in boiling lard, drain them well and serve them covered with sifted sugar.

A CHEAP BREAD PUDDING.

Take some slices of stale bread, free them from crust, and soak them well in cold water, which makes the pudding lighter than when hot water is used. Press out the superfluous water, add a little salt, grated ginger, sugar, nutmeg, and a few well-picked currants: mix the whole well together, lay it in a buttered dish, put a few pieces of butter on the top, and bake for forty minutes in a moderate oven.

GOOSEBERRY FOOL.

Plain bake your gooseberries in an oven, and, when they are quite soft, mash them well, and press them through a fine colander: put plenty of sugar to them, and, when cold, gradually mix them with equal parts of new milk and cream, first boiled together, and allowed to grow cold. Pour it into a dish, and serve. A little spice maybe added if preferred.

This is the ordinary manner of treating gooseberry fool; but the more elegant way is to half fill small china or custard cups with the plain sweetened fruit-pulp, then put in a thick layer of raw cream, and strew powdered spices thickly on the top. Serve as you would custards.

RASPBERRY FRITTERS.

Take the crumb of a penny-roll grated, add to it rather less than a pint of boiling milk: when this is cold, mix with it the beaten yolks of four eggs; sweeten it, and stir in sufficient fresh raspberry-juice to turn it an agreeable pink colour. Drop small spoonfuls of this batter into a pan of boiling lard, and, when done, stick them over with sliced blanched almonds.

A PLAIN BAKED PUDDING.

Boil a pint of new milk, then stir in flour enough to make it pretty thick; add three ounces of sugar, four ounces of fresh butter, the yolks of four eggs and the whites of two, a little salt, and a grated nutmeg. Mix the whole well together, lay it in a buttered dish, and bake it thirty minutes.

FRANGIPANNI TART.

Pound eight macaroons, pour sufficient boiling milk upon them to make them into a light batter; strain and beat six eggs, add them to the macaroons; sweeten it, and put it into a saucepan: stir it over the fire until it becomes of the requisite thickness. Put in four ounces of cream or fresh butter, and a tablespoonful of orange-flower water. Line the rim of a tart-dish with a puff-paste, lay in the frangipanni, put on a top crust, and bake for twenty minutes or half an hour, according to the heat of the oven.

RICE CUSTARDS.

Boil two or three bay-leaves and some bits of cinnamon and lemon-peel in a quart of new milk; then rub down a spoonful of ground rice in a little cold milk, add the beaten yolks of two eggs, gradually mix it with the boiled milk, straining the latter from the leaves, etc.; then put it over the fire in a saucepan, stir it gently until it thickens, pour it into a dish, stir in a spoonful of brandy, and, when cold, either put a whipped cream upon the top or serve in glass cups.

ALMOND PUDDING, BOILED.

Take an equal weight each of blanched sweet almonds, eggs, butter, flour, and sugar; pound them all well together in a mortar until a smooth paste is formed; then pour upon it sufficient hot milk to dilute it into a thin paste. Put it over the fire in a saucepan, stir it till of proper consistency; then lay it in a buttered basin, tie it down tight, and boil it for an hour.

OMELETTE AU CITRON.

Beat six eggs, well sweeten them, and add the grated rind of a lemon and a good teaspoonful of grated ginger; pour it into a frying-pan containing enough boiling lard, fry it on one side only, fold it, and serve upon a white napkin.

CHERRY PUDDING.

Pull your fruit from the stalks, and put it into a pudding-basin lined with a very rich suet-crust; strew in plenty of sugar, pour in a glass of brandy, cover it with a top crust, tie it down, and boil it for two hours.

REFORM CLUB PUDDING.

Separately whisk half a pound of fresh butter and the yolks of eight eggs until both form a snow, then beat them together, add a quarter of a pound of powdered loaf-sugar and a gill of brandy; line the inside of a tart-dish with a very thin paste, pour in the pudding, arrange some citron-chips on the top, and put it into a pretty quick oven for twenty minutes.

N.B.—This pudding, as well as most of those which have an under-crust, should be either lifted or turned out of the baking-dish to be served.

FRENCH PRUNE PUDDING.

Boil a quart of new milk; beat the yolks of six eggs and the whites of three; add two spoonsful of ground-ginger, a little salt, and four spoonsful of flour; gradually mix in the milk, stir it well up, throw in a pound of French dried prunes, tie it up in a cloth, boil it for an hour, and serve with melted butter poured over it when turned out.

PUDDINGS IN HASTE.

Take a quarter of a pound each of bread-crumbs, chopped suet, and cleaned currants, a little grated lemon-peel and ginger, and the yolks of four and the whites of two eggs: mix well together, and make into balls the size of a hen's egg. Throw them into boiling water, and in twenty minutes they will be done. Serve with sweet sauce.

JULY.

———

In this glorious month we have everything that heart of epicurean can wish for—odoriferous apricots, luscious raspberries, glowing cherries, refreshing currants, fully ripe gooseberries, blooming plums, gratefully cool strawberries, yea, even early apples, which offer themselves so temptingly to our attention, as almost to make it a meritorious thing for us to refrain from gathering them until the blessed Swithin's showers have consecrated them to our use. What matters it, then, if milk soon turns sour, or that butter is uneatable, and that, owing to the number of maternally-inclined hens, there is a falling off in our supply of eggs? We notice not the deficiency; for if everything abounded at the same time, we should only find that our enjoyment of the transient delights of summer time was inconveniently interfered with.

I must here say a word respecting two of the dishes of the month—tansy pudding and whortleberry pie—which have been stigmatized, the one as being nauseous, the other mawkish. Now, if well compounded, tansy pudding may challenge comparison with any other preparation ever invented; and whortleberry pie, seved with cider sauce and cream, is delicious beyond anything the rude multitude who has never tasted it can imagine.

PUDDINGS, ETC., FOR JULY.

Red-currant Pudding, baked.
Tourte de Cerises.
Tansy Pudding, baked.
Cherry Fritters.
Currant and Raspberry, or
   Currant and Cherry Pudding.
French Raspberry Tart.
Ripe Gooseberry Pudding.
Thyme Dumplings.
Black-currant Tart.
Cherry, or Strawberry Fool.
Croûtes aux Abricots.
Green Grape Tart.

Sponge Puddings.
Cherry and Currant Tart.
Quick-made Marrow Pudding.
Scalded Codlins.
Rice Custards without Eggs.
Bread-and-Butter Pudding,
   boiled.
Red or White Raspberry Fool.
Roussettes.
Cream Pudding, boiled.
Whortleberry Pie.
Tourte de Lorraine.
Sultana Pudding.

RED-CURRANT PUDDING, BAKED.

Red-currant pudding may be made in the usual way, with a pudding-crust and boiled; or it can be made by pressing the fruit through a sieve, so as to free it from the pips, which are very disagreeable; then, to a pint of pulp add two ounces of bread-crumbs and a quarter of a pound of sugar; put it into a tart-dish with a rim of puff-paste: serve with cream or custard. White currants may be treated in the same manner.

TOURTE DE CERISES.

Have a very shallow round tin tart-mould, not more than an inch and a half deep; cover it with a paste not thicker than a penny-piece, then take some fine cherries, cut off their stems with a pair of scissors so as not to tear the fruit—the principal beauty of a cherry tart consisting in the fruit being whole when sent to table. Pack in a single layer of the cherries; strew a good deal of sugar over them, and bake for three-quarters of an hour in a gentle oven. Serve hot or cold.

TANSY PUDDING, BAKED.

Beat four ounces of blanched almonds very fine in a mortar; add a little orange-flower water to prevent its oiling. Pour a pint of boiling hot cream upon a sliced French-roll; whisk four eggs; mix them with some sugar, a little grated nutmeg, a glass of brandy, and a very small quantity of tansy and spinach juice to give it a green colour. Put the almonds, French-roll, and other ingredients into a saucepan with a quarter of a pound of butter; stir it over the fire, and, when it gets thick, lay it in a tart-dish edged with a rim of very light paste: cover it with a top crust, and bake it for forty minutes.

CHERRY FRITTERS.

Take half a pound of ripe Mayduke cherries; stone and halve them: make a pint of new milk pretty hot, sweeten it, and pour it upon your cherries; then well beat four eggs, put them with the cherries, stir all well together, add a little flour to bind it; put it into a frying-pan a spoonful at a time, and when the fritters are done, serve with sugar sifted over them.

CURRANT AND RASPBERRY, OR CURRANT AND CHERRY PUDDING.

Take equal quantities of raspberries and currants, or cherries and currants; line a pudding-basin with a suet-crust; stem your fruit; put it into the basin with plenty of sugar, but do not put any water; cover it with a top crust well fastened on; tie a cloth over it, and boil for two hours.

FRENCH RASPBERRY TART.

Choose a pint of very fine ripe raspberries, either red or white; stem them, and throw them into a boiling syrup, made with a quarter of a pound of loaf-sugar and a tablespoonful of water; withdraw them immediately from the fire; line a tart-dish with a puff-paste rolled as thinly as possible; lay in the fruit and syrup, observing to keep the raspberries as whole as possible; put it into a quick oven for twenty minutes; strew more sugar over it, and glaze it; or, if to be served cold, pour raw cream over it.

RIPE GOOSEBERRY PUDDING.

Scald a pint of ripe gooseberries in very little water; when tender, mash them in the liquor in which they were boiled; pulp them through a sieve, and add to them the beaten yolks of four eggs, a quarter of a pound of sugar, and a quarter of a pound of blanched sweet almonds lightly chopped. Mix all very well together, and bake it in a pie-dish edged with a rim of puff-paste. Half an hour's baking will do it. Serve with cream.

THYME DUMPLINGS.

Well wash some sprigs of thyme; pick off, singly, a quarter of an ounce of the tender leaves; mix them with the crumb of a penny-roll grated, three-quarters of a pound of finely-shred beef-suet, a dessert-spoonful of sugar, four eggs well beaten, and enough brandy to make it the consistency of paste. Form it into dumplings; flour them well outside; put them into cloths, and boil them for three-quarters of an hour. Serve with wine sauce poured over them.

BLACK-CURRANT TART.

Lightly stem and top the currants, being careful not to bruise them; put them into a tart-dish with a rim of paste, and, as they are considered to be too rich by themselves, it is advisable to add a little white-currant juice or cider to dilute their flavour: throw in a good deal of sugar, cover them with a top crust, and bake rather more than an hour.

CHERRY OR STRAWBERRY FOOL.

Pick the stems from your fruit; if cherries, stone them, bruise them to a pulp, add a sufficiency of loaf-sugar pounded and sifted, and half a pint of cream to a pint of pulp; put it into custard-glasses with a layer of raw cream upon the top, and serve.—Some housekeepers, to avoid the trouble of frequent bakings, line several tart-dishes with an edge of crust: bake them and keep them for use as required, when some preserve or raw fruit as above may be simply laid in, and an easy-made tart produced upon an emergency.

CROÛTES AUX ABRICOTS.

Halve and stone some apricots; place each half with the inside uppermost upon a thin square-shaped piece of bread; fit them into the bottom of a well-buttered tart-dish, lay a piece of butter upon each, sprinkle them with sugar, and bake them for half an hour in a moderate oven; when done, arrange them carefully in a dish, pour over them the syrup they made in cooking, and serve hot. Peaches, large plums, and pears may be done thus.

GREEN-GRAPE TART.

In this month the out-of-door grape-vines are generally thinned of their fruit: take the grapes when they are no larger than sweet-pea seed, and clarify some sugar; throw in the grapes, simmer them for about five minutes, put a rim of rich crust round your dish, lay in your fruit and syrup, cover with a top crust, and bake for forty minutes. Serve with a custard.

SPONGE PUDDINGS.

Beat a quarter of a pound of fresh butter until it creams, add to it two ounces of powdered and sifted sugar, two tablespoonsful of flour, a dessert-spoonful of brandy, and four eggs, first beaten and then strained. Mix all well together, butter six small cups, put the pudding into them, and bake them for twenty minutes.

CHERRY AND CURRANT TART.

Stem and stone your cherries: take an equal weight of very ripe red currants, press them through a sieve, add the juice to your cherries with the crumb of two penny sponge-cakes, a quarter of a pound of sugar, and a wineglassful of brandy. Put it into a tart-dish lined with a rim of paste, cover it with a top crust, and bake it for an hour.

QUICK-MADE MARROW PUDDING.

Take the crumb of a penny-roll, pour over it half a pint of boiling milk, stir it well together, and when cold, add a pound of beef-marrow finely shred, four eggs well beaten, a glass of brandy, and sugar and nutmeg to taste; mix the whole thoroughly together, put it into a pie-dish, and bake it for forty minutes. Stick a few chips of candied-peel over it before serving.

SCALDED CODLINS.

Choose some middling-sized codlins; wrap each in a vine-leaf, and pack them closely together in the bottom of a saucepan:

pour in enough water to cover them; set them upon the fire and simmer them slowly until done enough to take the skin off when cold: arrange them in a dish, strew plenty of white sugar over them, and pour in some rich cream.

RICE CUSTARDS WITHOUT EGGS.

Take seven teacupsful of new milk and one teacupful of whole rice, put it into a bain-marie, or in a jar placed to stand in a pot of boiling water, which must be kept boiling until the rice is boiled perfectly smooth; then sweeten it with pounded loaf-sugar; mix in two ounces of blanched sweet almonds beaten to a paste, and when cold, put it into your cups and serve.

BREAD-AND-BUTTER PUDDING, BOILED.

Take a round sandwich loaf; begin to cut from the top some slices of bread; butter them, strew some sugar upon them, beat four eggs, dip your bread into them, and lay the slices in a basin, with the buttered side downwards; when the basin is about three parts full, pour in a pint of milk in which you have boiled two bitter almonds, and, when cold, and the bread properly swelled, tie a well-floured cloth over it, and boil for an hour. Pour melted butter over it when served.

RED OR WHITE RASPBERRY FOOL.

Put your fruit for a quarter of an hour into an oven; when tender, pulp it through a sieve, sugar it, add the crumb of sufficient sponge-cake to thicken it; put it into a glass mould, or into custard-cups, and lay some thick cream on the top. If for immediate use, the cream may be beaten up with the fruit.

ROUSSETTES.

Take ten ounces of flour, make a pit in the middle of it; stir in two eggs, two ounces of butter melted, two ounces of powdered loaf-sugar, and a little luke-warm milk; mix it well, and let it stand for three hours, then roll it out as thin as a penny-piece, cut it into neat lozenge-shaped pieces the size of a jam-tart; fry these in a very hot friture until they are of a good deep brown; drain them, and serve with a few brandy-cherries upon each.

CREAM PUDDING, BOILED.

Take a pint of sweet cream, boil it with a blade of mace and a little nutmeg, then strain it, and let it stand to cool. Beat the yolks of four eggs and the whites of two, mix with them a dessert-spoonful of flour, two ounces of blanched sweet-almonds, pounded to a paste, and a spoonful of orange-flower water. Gradually mix these ingredients with the cream, beat it up well, take a doubled cloth, wet and well flour it, pour in the pudding, tie it tight, and boil it for twenty minutes in a good deal of water. When done, turn it into a dish, and pour over it melted butter and sugar.

WHORTLEBERRY PIE.

Whortleberries are usually accompanied by mazzards, or small black cherries, which are used to give more flavour to the first-named fruit, but a few sharp apples cut exceedingly thin, or a little cider added to the whortleberries, does just as well. Put a rim of paste round your dish, lay in your fruit, warm up a little rough cider and sugar, pour it over your pie, put on a top lid of crust, and bake in a moderate oven for an hour.

TOURTE DE LORRAINE.

Mix a pound of fine dry flour with four eggs, a quarter of a pound of butter, and a little salt; roll it out rather less than an inch thick, turn up the edges, or, if easier, put it into a shallow tart-mould, place it in the oven, and at the end of twenty minutes take it out and fill it with a pint of thick cream, three eggs, and two tablespoonfuls of either raspberry or cherry juice well beaten together; add a few pieces of butter here and there, put it into the oven again, and let it bake for twenty minutes. Serve with sugar sifted over it.

SULTANA PUDDING.

Soak two ounces of sultana raisins in enough brandy to cover them. Take half a pound of flour, half a pound of chopped suet, a dessert-spoonful of ground ginger, two eggs, four ounces of white sugar and enough milk to make it a pretty light paste; add the raisins and brandy, put it into a cloth or basin, boil it for two hours, and serve with what pudding sauce you please.

AUGUST.

ALREADY the summer tide is ebbing gently; but although the days are palpably decreasing, our appetites and our digestions proportionably improve and what inexhaustible attractions the season possesses! The full-flavoured fruits of August are of the richest and the most mellow kind: the many-coloured plums are in their prime, and fragrant apricots, savoury greengages, juicy pears, painted nectarines, blush-cheeked peaches, and bland, unctuous figs, appear in all their pomp at our desserts, while the fruits of humbler growth, such as apples and late cherries, are left to be on active service as entremets upon our dinner-tables; and the almost total disappearance of winter fruits from our stores gives us full leisure to apply ourselves to the enjoyment of the produce of our own gardens; and in the agreeable asperity of our English fruits we find wherewith to refresh our palates, in readiness for the more cloying fruits of other countries, which very soon will be consigned to our shores.

PUDDINGS, ETC., FOR AUGUST.

Black-currant Pudding.

Custard Pudding, boiled.

Apricot Pudding.

Cream Pudding, baked.

Apple Dumplings, boiled or baked.

Cherry-and-Almond Pudding.

Veal-suet Pudding, baked or
  boiled.

Apple Pudding.

Imperial Pudding.

Syllabub Pudding.

Bitter-almond Custards.

Codlin Pie.

Potato Pudding, boiled.

Porcupine Pudding.

Sweet Egg Pie.

Ratafia Pudding.

Greengage Pudding or Tart.

Pommes au Beurre.

Calves'-feet Pudding.

Tapioca Pudding.

The Derby Pudding.

Frangipanni Pudding.

Yorkshire Pudding.

Gipsy Pudding

BLACK-CURRANT PUDDING.

In backward seasons black-currants are plentiful until nearly the middle of August. Stem your fruit, but you need not top them. Line a pudding-basin with a light paste; strew sugar over it; then put in your black-currants; add more sugar and a teacupful of cider, or an apple or two sliced thin; cover with a top crust; tie a cloth over it, and boil for two hours.

N.B. Never put water with fruit puddings or pies: lemon-juice, grape-juice, or cider is admissible, but water should on no account be used.

CUSTARD PUDDING, BOILED.

From a pint of cream take a teacupful; mix it with a tablespoonful of fine flour. Set the remainder of the cream on the fire to boil, and as soon as it has boiled, take it off and stir in the moistened flour; when cool, add the beaten yolks of five eggs and the whites of two, a glass of white wine, a little nutmeg, and sugar to taste; mix all well together; butter a basin, pour in the pudding, tie a well-floured cloth over it, and boil it for half an hour. Turn it into a dish to serve, and pour melted butter over it.

APRICOT PUDDING.

Apricots may be made into a pudding in the ordinary way by first pushing out the stones, and then putting the fruit into a pudding-basin lined with suet-crust, covering it with a lid of paste, and boiling it for an hour or more, according to size. Or you can stone the apricots and coddle them until they are soft, then break them into small pieces, and, when cold, mix them with the yolks of four eggs and the whites of two, a pint of good cream, and a sufficiency of sugar. Mix all together, pour it into a tart-dish lined with a puff-paste, and bake for half an hour; when done, lift it out of the dish, and sift sugar over it. If you have but few apricots, some apples cut into thin slices will eke them out and make an agreeable mixture.

CREAM PUDDING, BAKED.

Well whisk the yolks of six eggs and the whites of two; add two ounces of powdered white sugar, a tablespoonful of very good Marsala, two ounces of pounded ratafia cakes, and two ounces of sultana raisins soaked in wine. Boil a pint of rich cream; mix it gradually with the other ingredients; put it into a tart-dish lined with a very light puff-paste; place it in a moderate oven, and bake it for twenty minutes.

APPLE DUMPLINGS, BOILED OR BAKED.

Choose some sizeable codlins, or other good boiling apples; pare, but do not core them: make some rich suet-crust; roll it out moderately thin; wrap each apple in enough to cover it; fasten the edge of the paste securely by wetting it slightly; tie them in cloths, or merely flour the outsides; throw them into boiling water, and boil them about forty minutes; serve with melted butter and sugar. If baked, they should not be floured after they are made, but laid in a dish, and baked for nearly an hour in a slow oven. Cold boiled dumplings eat well if warmed up by baking them for thirty minutes.

CHERRY-AND-ALMOND PUDDING.

Line a shallow tart-mould with a thin light paste; stone a pound of ripe cherries; lay them in and put plenty of sugar with them. Then take a quarter of a pound of blanched almonds; cut them into quarters; strew them amongst your cherries; sift sugar over, and bake for an hour in a gentle oven. This is equally good hot or cold.

VEAL-SUET PUDDING, BAKED OR BOILED.

Chop half a pound of veal-suet; put it into a quart of rich new milk; set it upon the fire, and, when pretty hot, pour it upon eight ounces of bread-crumbs, and sugar to your taste; add half a pound of currants washed and dried, and three well-beaten eggs; put it into a floured cloth or buttered dish, and either boil or bake it an hour.

APPLE PUDDING.

Make a very good suet-crust; roll it out flat; pare, core, and cut up your apples; put them in a heap upon the paste; throw in a good deal of sugar; close the whole carefully, and boil it tied in a cloth. Two hours will do it. When done, lift a bit of the crust, lay in a good bit of butter, replace the crust, and send to table as hot as possible. In this manner fruit puddings of every description may be made for family consumption.

IMPERIAL PUDDING.

Put four ounces of fine bread-crumbs to soak in some raw milk, and the same quantity of bread to soak in a strong infusion of saffron. Drain both; separate the yolks and whites of six eggs; beat each for a quarter of an hour, then add the yolks to the bread soaked in saffron, and the whites to that soaked in milk; take a good-sized pudding-mould; butter it and put in alternate layers of the soaked bread, and between each strew citron chips and chopped sweet almonds: pour over it half a pint of sweetened cream; tie it over with a floured cloth, and boil it for an hour. Turn it out to serve, and pour wine-sauce in the dish. The Queen of Spain's pudding is made by using rice instead of bread-crumbs, and interspersing the layers with fruits preserved in brandy, some of which are also used to decorate the dish in which the pudding is served.

SYLLABUB PUDDING.

Well beat your eggs; add to them six ounces of pounded and sifted loaf-sugar, a glass of brandy, a glass of white wine, and sufficient flour to make it a very stiff batter. Have a quart of milk warm from the cow poured upon it while you continue beating; and when it is well frothed, put it into a buttered dish; place it in a quick oven, and bake it for a quarter of an hour. Serve immediately.

BITTER-ALMOND CUSTARDS.

Boil two or three bitter almonds in a pint of new milk; gradually add the yolks of four eggs, beaten and strained: remove the almonds, and either boil or bake the custards.

CODLIN PIE.

Put some small codlins into a glazed saucepan, lay vine-leaves over them, and add enough water to cover them: place them by the side of a very slow fire; keep the steam from escaping, and when they are nicely greened, take them out, arrange them in a dish with plenty of powdered loaf-sugar; put a rim of paste round the dish and a top of light crust. Bake for an hour. Either serve with a custard apart, or when done, lift the crust and pour a custard over the fruit.

POTATO PUDDING, BOILED.

Boil four large floury potatoes till they are thoroughly done; peel them and mash them smooth with the back of a spoon; mix them with enough milk to enable you to rub them through a sieve, then add six ounces of butter, first melted, four ounces of sugar, a wine-glass of brandy, four well-beaten eggs, and a quarter of a pound of washed currants. Put it into a buttered mould, and boil it for forty minutes. Serve with wine sauce poured over it.

PORCUPINE PUDDING.

Boil half a pound of rice in a quart of new milk and one ounce of butter; when tender, let it cool: then add a spoonful of laurel-water, sugar to your taste, and six well-beaten eggs. Mix the whole well together; put it into a mould, and boil it an hour and twenty minutes. Turn it into your dish, and stick it over with slit almonds. Serve, surrounded by a rich custard.

SWEET EGG PIE.

Cover a pie-dish with a rich paste; then take twelve hard-boiled eggs, lay them in the dish, throw in half a pound of butter cut up, and half a pound of well-cleaned currants: beat up four eggs in half a pint of white wine, sweeten it well, pour it in, put on a top crust, and bake it for half an hour.

RATAFIA PUDDING.

Boil two or three laurel-leaves in a pint of cream; then take them out, and stir in a quarter of a pound of butter, a quarter of a pound of grated biscuit, a glass of white wine, a little nutmeg and a sufficiency of sugar. Take it off the fire, cover it up, and when nearly cold, put in two ounces of blanched sweet-almonds and the yolks of four eggs. Mix all well together; put it into a dish, and bake half an hour.

GREENGAGE PUDDING OR TART.

Take some greengage plums, not over-ripe: do not stone them, but lay them either in a basin lined, or pie-dish edged, with a rich crust; add a good quantity of white sugar, cover with a top crust, and boil or bake for an hour and a half.

POMMES AU BEURRE.

Peel some good-dressing apples, core them from the top without cutting them through; butter a tart-dish; line it with as many pieces of bread as you have apples; place an apple upon each; put some pounded loaf-sugar and a bit of butter into each. Lay them in an oven; renew the butter and sugar occasionally, and bake until the apples are done and the bread looks nice and brown.

CALVES'-FEET PUDDING.

Mince very fine half a pound of the flesh of calves' feet, then take twelve ounces of fine beef-suet, chopped small and freed from the hard parts, the yolks of four eggs, four ounces of grated bread, half a pound of clean-picked currants, a tablespoonful of flour, half a grated nutmeg, and sugar to your taste. Boil it in a cloth for five hours. Turn it into a dish to serve, and pour white-wine sauce over it.

TAPIOCA PUDDING.

Take a teacupful of fine large tapioca; wash it in cold water, and lay it to soak for six hours in a quart of new milk: then put it over the fire and stir until quite soft; add two ounces of butter, a little spice; sugar to the taste, and two well-beaten eggs mixed with a little cream or cold milk; put it into a well-buttered dish, with or without a rim of crust, and bake for half an hour.

A very elegant variation to this kind of pudding is made by first putting a good deal of marmalade into the dish, and pouring the tapioca, sago, or other substance over it.

THE DERBY PUDDING.

Beat a quarter of a pound of butter to a cream; whisk four eggs to a snow; add to them a quarter of a pound of powdered loaf-sugar, a little orange-flower water, and the beaten butter; then stir in three ounces of fine dry flour. Mix all well together; put it into a basin, and boil or bake it for an hour.

FRANGIPANNI PUDDING.

Pound four macaroons; add to them four ounces of bread-crumbs, four beaten eggs, two ounces of sugar, a glass of eau-de-vie, and enough cream to make it a stiff batter. Mix well together; put it into a mould or cloth, and boil for one hour. Serve with saffron sauce.

YORKSHIRE PUDDING.

This pudding is usually baked in front of the fire under roasting-meat; but it may be done in an oven as other puddings. Take three eggs and three tablespoonsful of flour, a glass of brandy, and a little sugar; beat these together for a quarter of an hour, then gradually add a quart of new milk, put it into a square tray, lay some bits of butter upon it, place it in a quick oven, and as soon as it is well browned on the top, cut it into square pieces, turn them, and when done, arrange them in a dish well covered with sifted loaf-sugar.

GIPSY PUDDING.

Cut some thin slices of stale bread; spread one side thickly with jam of any kind; pack them into a buttered tart-dish, and pour over them the yolks of six eggs beaten up in a gill of French brandy. Bake for twenty minutes, and sift sugar over it before serving.

SEPTEMBER.

THE commencement of the shooting-season naturally suggests to the epicure the interesting question of what pudding goes best with game? The answer generally is, that almost any pudding may be satisfactorily introduced when game has once made its appearance upon our dinner-tables. However, as we all have our preferences, I may as well acknowledge that in my opinion few things follow each other with more agreeable propriety than does a bread pudding succeed a brace of roasted partridges. Some people may pronounce in favour of a pippin tart, others make choice of pumpkin pie or damson pudding; but I still maintain that there is something in the simplicity of a bread pudding, which accords better with the condition of satisfaction in which the palate is left after partaking of game, than any more savoury or appetizing composition yet propounded by cook or gourmet. Next to a bread pudding I would recommend—by way of contrast to dessert fruits which are now so plentiful—a macaroni, sago, pearl barley, or many other equally desirable puddings which are to be found in the *menu* of the month.

PUDDINGS, ETC., FOR SEPTEMBER.

Rich Bread Pudding, boiled.

Pumpkin Pie.

Damson Pudding, baked

Harvest Pudding.

Pippin Tart.

Rice Small Puddings.

The Friars' Omelet.

Potato Pudding, baked.

Poires à l'Allemande.

Macaroni Pudding, baked.

Honey Pudding.

Pearl Barley Pudding.

White Pudding.

Blackberry Tart or Pudding.

Dutch Pudding.

Apple Fool.

Ginger Pudding.

Beignets de Pommes ou de Pêches.

Sago Pudding, baked.

Sardinian Pudding.

Damson Tart.

Biscuit Pudding, baked,

Omelette aux Amandes.

RICH BREAD PUDDING, BOILED.

Blanch two bitter almonds, pound them in a mortar, and add them to a pint of new milk and sufficient bread-crumbs to soak up the milk; let it stand an hour, then add the beaten yolks of four eggs and the whites of two, a quarter of a pound of washed currants, two ounces of butter, two ounces of sugar, and a little spice. Mix all well together; put it into a buttered basin, and boil it for an hour. When done, turn it into a dish; pour wine sauce over it, and thickly strew it with pounded loaf-sugar.

PUMPKIN PIE.

Peel your pumpkin, take away the seeds, then cut it into small pieces, and put it into a saucepan with a tablespoonful of water or cider at the bottom: when tender, mash it very smooth, and while warm, stir in a quarter of a pound of fresh butter, the yolks of eight eggs well beaten, some nutmeg, half an ounce of grated ginger, sugar to taste, and enough cream to lighten it. Bake it in a dish lined with a paste, and cover it with a top crust. An hour and a half will do it.

DAMSON PUDDING, BAKED.

From a quart of milk take a few spoonsful, and beat in it the yolks of six eggs and the whites of three, four spoonsful of flour, a little salt, and two teaspoonsful of ground ginger. Then by degrees mix in the remainder of the milk, and a pint of sound ripe damsons. Boil it an hour tied in a well-floured cloth. Serve with melted butter over it.

HARVEST PUDDING.

Boil two or three bay-leaves in a pint of new milk, then remove the leaves and pour the hot milk upon a pint of sifted bread-crumbs; add six well-beaten eggs, and three ounces of honey. Thickly butter a basin; stick upon it bunches of red cranberries or slips of candied-peel cut into short lengths; stir in half a pint of cream with your pudding: mix well; put it into the basin; tie it down with a cloth, and boil it for two hours; turn it into a dish, and serve it, decorated with two or three ears of corn stuck into it.

PIPPIN TART.

Take six good-sized pippins and six large tomatoes; peel, core, and cut up the pippins; put them into a glazed saucepan; squeeze the pulp from the tomatoes; put it with the apples; add a quarter of a pound of white sugar, and stir it over the fire until the apples begin to feel tender; then put an edge of puff-paste round a tart-dish; lay in your fruit, stirring in a couple of tablespoonsful of rich cream as you do so. Cover it with crust; place it in a moderately brisk oven, and bake for twenty minutes.

RICE SMALL PUDDINGS.

Wash a teacupful of rice and put it to simmer in half a pint of milk; when it is pretty thick, pour in a breakfast-cupful of thick cream, and let it come to a boil. Retire it to get cold, then mix it with the yolks of four eggs and the whites of two; sugar it to taste; add a little nutmeg and candied-peel; butter small cups, three parts fill them, and bake for thirty minutes in a moderate oven. Turn out upon a dish, and serve quickly with sweet sauce.

THE FRIARS' OMELET.

Bake some fine large apples, peel them, and take a pint of their pulp, freed from core; mash it up with four ounces each of fresh butter and loaf-sugar in powder, and, as soon as cold, add four eggs well beaten; then take a tart-dish, butter it thoroughly, and strew it over with a thick coating of bread-crumbs; put in the ingredients; strew more bread-crumbs on the top, and bake it forty minutes. Turn it out to serve, and dust it over well with pounded lump-sugar.

POTATO PUDDING, BAKED.

Boil one pound of very mealy potatoes; peel and beat them in a mortar, then add four ounces of pounded and sifted loaf-sugar, four ounces of butter first melted, a quarter of a pint of white wine, the yolks of four eggs and the whites of two, and a little nutmeg. Lay a puff-paste over your dish; put in the pudding, and bake it till it is of a fine brown colour.

POIRES À L'ALLEMANDE.

Peel some dressing pears; cut them in quarters; take out the pips and shake the pears in a frying-pan over the fire with a small quantity of butter; dredge flour over them; add a little wine and sugar, and simmer them till they are tender; thicken the sauce with some yolk of egg, and serve hot.

MACARONI PUDDING, BAKED.

Take a quarter of a pound of Naples macaroni, swell it in milk with a pinch of saffron and sugar to taste; when soft, stir in a quarter of a pound of fresh butter and a glass of French brandy, put it into a buttered pie-dish edged with a rim of crust, pour two beaten eggs over it, and bake for half an hour.

HONEY PUDDING.

Take half a pound of clear honey, half a pint of grape-juice, four eggs, and half a pound of butter beaten to a cream; add two ounces of bread-crumbs, beat all together for ten minutes; put it into a buttered mould, and boil it for an hour and a half. If you have not the grape-juice, you can employ rather more than half a pint of either Morello cherries, damsons, or harvest plums, stoned.

PEARL BARLEY PUDDING.

Wash half a pound of pearl barley quite clean; put it into a deep pan with three pints of new milk, a quarter of a pound of loaf-sugar, and half a nutmeg grated; lay it in a bread-oven, and when properly swelled, take it out; beat up four eggs; mix all well together; butter a pudding-basin; pour in your pudding; tie it down with a floured cloth, and boil it for an hour.

WHITE PUDDING.

Boil a quarter of a pound of ground rice in rather more than a pint of milk, until it is quite smooth, then beat four ounces of blanched sweet almonds until they form a paste. Wash and dry a quarter of a pound of currants; chop half a pound of beef-suet; beat three eggs; add a quarter of a pound of white sugar, and a grated nutmeg. Mix all well together, and boil in a floured cloth for one hour. Serve with warmed cream poured over it.

BLACKBERRY TART OR PUDDING.

As the pips of this fruit are very indigestible, it is advisable only to use the pulp of the ripe blackberries. Take a pint of pulp, a glass of brandy, six sharp apples, pared, cored, and cut small, a grated biscuit, and, if possible, a handful of sloes; mix well together; sweeten to taste, and either make it into a tart or pudding. Dress it an hour, and serve with a custard or cream.

DUTCH PUDDING.

Warm half a pint of new milk; melt half a pound of fresh butter in it, and let it stand until it is almost cold; then strain it into a pound of flour; add two large spoonsful of yeast, and four eggs well beaten; mix it very well together, and let it stand in a warm place for an hour to rise; then stir into it a quarter of a pound of moist-sugar, half a pound of sultana raisins, and two glasses of Hollands; put it into a square tray well buttered, and bake for forty minutes. Serve turned out into a dish.

APPLE FOOL.

Put some baking-apples into a slow oven, and, when they are soft enough, peel them and pulp them through a sieve; add plenty of sugar and pounded spice; boil together a sufficiency of new milk and cream, and when cold, mix it with the fruit, and serve either in small cups or in a mould.

GINGER PUDDING.

Take two ounces of preserved ginger; put it into a mortar; beat it to a paste; add the crumb of two penny sponge-cakes, or their equivalent of grated bread, the yolks of four eggs, and the whites of two, two ounces of sugar, and half a pint of cream; beat all together; butter a mould; stick some small slips of preserved ginger over it; lay in your pudding; tie it down with a cloth, and boil it for one hour.

BEIGNETS DE POMMES OU DE PÊCHES.

Peel your apples or peaches; core or stone them; and cut them into tolerably thick slices; put them to soak in brandy and sugar; let them remain upon the hob or over a slow fire for a few minutes; then drain them and dip them in batter; fry them over a quick fire, and serve with sifted sugar strewed over them.

SAGO PUDDING, BAKED.

Boil three dessert-spoonsful of sago in rather more than a pint of new milk, with some cinnamon, nutmeg, and sugar: when well thickened, mix in three beaten eggs; lay a puff-paste round your dish; put in the sago, and bake it for forty minutes. A plainer way is to wash a good tablespoonful of sago, and put it into a buttered pie-dish; pour a quart of milk over it; sweeten it; add a little spice, and place it in a moderate oven for an hour and a half.

SARDINIAN PUDDING.

Take some small green figs; place them in a tart-dish well buttered; strew them over with sugar; then boil a quart of new milk until it is reduced to nearly one half; add a little butter to it; sweeten to taste, and pour it upon the figs: place them in a very slow oven for forty minutes. If the milk is properly reduced at first, it will be a very rich custard when the pudding is done.

DAMSON TART.

Damsons being a very rich fruit, require a few apples to lower them. Take equal quantities of fine ripe damsons and sliced apples; mix them together; add plenty of sugar, or honey, which is far preferable, and bake in a pie-dish edged with paste; cover it with a lid of the same, and bake for an hour and a half.

BISCUIT PUDDING, BAKED.

Take four small-sized hard biscuits, and four macaroons; pound them well in a mortar; sift them, and pour over them half a pint each of hot cream and new milk; stir well till nearly cold; then add a quarter of a pound of powdered loaf-sugar, the yolks of six eggs and the whites of four, and a spoonful of orange-flower water; mix thoroughly; put it into a pie-dish, with or without a rim of puff-paste, and bake for an hour.

OMELETTE AUX AMANDES.

Take six eggs, beat them well and add to them two ounces of sugar and a quarter of a pound of blanched sweet almonds reduced to a paste; mix well together; fry it quickly, and serve with spiced sugar. N.B.—All omelettes should be folded double before sending to table, by which means they are lighter than if laid flat in the dish.

OCTOBER.

As autumn comes round, the calls upon our hospitality daily press more and more heavily upon us; and now, in the hunting month of October, it seems that our whole thoughts should be devoted to the entertainment of not only those whose pheasants, hares, and partridges dignify our tables, but the less fortunate of our friends, who only own to a very distant acquaintance with these aristocratic eatables.

In October every one's appetite is in good order; and whether our *convives* consist of the proverbially hungry hunter, or more soberly-inclined bodies, we have the satisfaction to find that at this season ample honour is done to the provisions we set before them.

PUDDINGS, ETC., FOR OCTOBER.

Scotch Apple Pie.

Brown Bread Pudding.

Marlborough Pudding.

Black Cap Pudding.

Bullace, or Harvest Plum Pudding.

Biscuit Pudding, boiled.

Quince Tart.

Potato Suet Pudding.

Cranberry Tart or Pudding.

American Oatmeal Pudding.

Eve's Pudding.

Chestnut Pudding, boiled.

Clarence Pudding.

Carrot Pudding, baked.

Fine Hasty Pudding.

Berkshire Apple Dumplings.

Pear Tart.

Rose Custards.

Rich Rice Pudding, baked.

Apple Fritters.

Chocolate Pudding.

Puff Pudding.

Crit Tarts.

Zouave Pudding.

SCOTCH APPLE PIE.

Take a dozen good baking-apples; peel, core, and cut them up small; put an edge of crust to a pie-dish; throw in some sugar at the bottom, then put in your apples, and lay half a pot of Scotch marmalade on the top; cover with a lid of crust, and bake for an hour.

BROWN BREAD PUDDING.

Take half a pound of good brown bread without crust; cut it into moderately thin slices; spread them over with cream; lay them in a buttered dish; strew finely-shred candied citron-peel between each slice; boil half a pint of new milk; add some sugar and cinnamon; pour it over the bread, and when nearly cold, beat three eggs and pour into the dish. Bake for half an hour in a moderately-heated oven.

MARLBOROUGH PUDDING.

Line a tart-dish with a very thin paste; then take one ounce each of candied lemon, orange, and citron peel, sliced exceeding thin; lay these at the bottom of the dish; then melt over the fire six ounces of butter; add six ounces of powdered loaf-sugar, the yolks of four eggs well beaten, and a dessert-spoonful of orange-flower water: pour these ingredients over the sweetmeats, and bake for three-quarters of an hour.

BLACK CAP PUDDING.

Take a pint of new milk; mix into it by degrees three tablespoon-fuls of fine dry flour; strain and simmer it over the fire until pretty thick; then add two ounces of butter; let it grow cold, and stir in the yolks of four eggs beaten and strained, and half a pound of currants washed and dried. Put it into a well-floured cloth; tie it tight; place it in boiling water; move it about a little to prevent its settling, and boil it one hour and a half. Serve with sweet sauce poured over it.

BULLACE, OR HARVEST PLUM PUDDING.

Line a basin with a good pudding-crust, not too thick; put in your fruit with plenty of sugar, and a teacupful of cider. Cover it with a crust, and boil it for two hours. If you have honey instead of sugar with any kind of plum pudding, it makes it much more delicious.

BISCUIT PUDDING, BOILED.

Boil a pint of new milk; pour it upon three penny Naples biscuits, grated; cover it close, and when cold, add the beaten yolks of four eggs and the whites of two, a dessert-spoonful of flour, and sugar to taste: boil it for one hour in a buttered basin, and serve with egg sauce.

QUINCE TART.

Choose your quinces quite ripe, peel and cut them into quarters, but do not core them; put them into a jar with some sugar and sufficient grape-juice to prevent their being dry. Place them in an oven, and let them do slowly until tender, then line your tart-dish with a rim of paste; put in your fruit and syrup; cover it with a top crust, and bake for forty minutes.

Remember, whether for tarts or for preserving, never put spices with quinces.

POTATO SUET PUDDING.

Take a pound of mealy potatoes boiled and mashed smooth; add four ounces of chopped beef-suet, three eggs, a little milk, sugar to taste, and a good dessert-spoonful of powdered ginger. Put it into a well-floured cloth and boil for an hour. Serve, turned into a dish, with saffron or sweet sauce poured over it.

CRANBERRY TART OR PUDDING.

Take half a pint of cranberries, pick them from their stems and throw them into a saucepan with half a pound of white sugar and a spoonful of water; let them come to a boil; then retire them to stand on the hob while you peel and cut up four large apples; put a rim of light paste round your dish; strew in the apples; pour the cranberries over them; cover with a lid of crust, and bake for an hour. For a pudding, proceed in the same manner with the fruit, and boil it in a basin or cloth.

AMERICAN OATMEAL PUDDING.

Take half a pint of whole groats; steep them over night in a pint of boiled milk; next morning take a quarter of a pound of shred beef-suet, some nutmeg, two ounces of washed currants, two ounces of sultana raisins, sufficient sugar to sweeten it, a very little salt, and two eggs well beaten. Stir all well together; tie it close in a floured cloth, and boil it two hours. Pour melted butter over it to serve.

EVE'S PUDDING.

Take half a pound each of grated bread, shred suet, chopped apples, and washed currants; add some nutmeg, a little sugar, and three eggs: mix the whole well together; put it into a pudding-mould, and boil for two hours. Serve with sweet sauce.

CHESTNUT PUDDING, BOILED.

Boil a dozen chestnuts in water for ten minutes; then peel them carefully so as not to break them; cut them into halves; pour a little essence of lemon upon them, and sprinkle them with sugar. Pound four ounces of hard biscuits, and let them soak in as much milk as they will retain; drain them, and add the beaten yolks of six eggs, two ounces of sugar, and a quarter of a pound of butter, first melted. Stir the ingredients well together, then lightly add the chestnuts; put it into a buttered basin; tie it well down, and boil it an hour.

CLARENCE PUDDING.

Butter a mould and cover it with sweetmeats of different kinds arranged in a pattern. Cut three sponge-cakes into slices; wet them with brandy: place them round the mould; then make a custard with a pint of new milk and two ounces of pounded sweet almonds; pour it over the sponge-cakes; cover it with a thickly-floured cloth; tie it down tight, and boil it for an hour.

CARROT PUDDING, BAKED.

Take half a pound of grated raw carrot, half a pound of bread-crumbs, the yolks of four eggs and the whites of two, a little sugar and nutmeg, a gill each of white wine and cream; mix all well together, lay a puff-paste over your dish; put in your pudding and bake for an hour.

FINE HASTY PUDDING.

Work an egg in enough flour to form a very stiff paste, then mince it as small as possible; put it into a quart of boiling milk, add some sugar, beaten cinnamon, and one ounce of butter; stir it one way until it is sufficiently thick; then put in another ounce of butter, pour it into your pie-dish; stick some bits of butter about the top, and bake it for half an hour.

BERKSHIRE APPLE DUMPLINGS.

Peel and core six middling-sized apples; cover them well over with white sugar; place them in a deep dish, and put them into your oven: when they become tender, pour over them a batter made with two eggs, two spoonsful of flour, and sufficient milk to make it of the requisite consistency. Bake for twenty minutes, and serve with spiced sugar, apart.

PEAR TART.

Take some dressing-pears; and as you peel them rub them in sugar to prevent their turning black; cut them into quarters, lay them in a tart-dish edged with a rim of light paste; add a gill of claret and some powdered loaf-sugar. Cover with a top crust and bake in a slow oven for an hour and a half. It is a great mistake to put spices with fresh fruit of any kind—a few cloves or a little mace tend rather to augment the insipidity than to refresh the flavour of even apples and pears; of course an exception is made in regard to fruit *fools*, which generally require spices.

ROSE CUSTARDS.

Take six ounces of dressed beetroot; pound it in a mortar until perfectly smooth; add enough rose-water to make it pass through a sieve; strain into it the whites of three eggs, beaten, and a pint of thick cream; stir it over the fire until sufficiently thick; then serve in custard-cups or in a glass dish.

RICH RICE PUDDING, BAKED.

Well wash half a pound of Carolina rice; swell it in water until tender; let it cool; add to it a quarter of a pint of cream, the yolks of five eggs and the whites of three, half a pound of marrow, a glass of brandy, half a pound of currants washed and picked, a quarter of a pound of sugar, and a dessert-spoonful of ratafia. Mix the whole well together; put an edge of crust round your dish; lay in the pudding, and bake in a moderate oven for forty minutes.

APPLE FRITTERS.

There are several ways of making apple fritters. You may peel, core, and cut some rounds of apple; dip them into batter and fry them; or you can mince the apples very fine, add sugar, drop some spoonsful of batter into a frying-pan, and place some chopped apple upon each. Another manner is to take the pulp of some baked apples, sugar it, and add it to an equal quantity of good stiff batter; fry them over a smart fire, and serve with spiced sugar.

CHOCOLATE PUDDING.

Scrape two ounces of French chocolate; add two ounces of powdered loaf-sugar, two ounces of very fine bread-crumbs, half a pint of cream, and the yolks of four and the whites of two eggs: beat the whole well together for ten minutes; butter a basin; put in your pudding, and boil it one hour. When done, turn it into a dish, and throw pounded sugar over it.

PUFF PUDDING.

Cut some stale white bread into thin slices; pour boiling milk upon, it, and let it stand till cold; then add four eggs, a little ratafia, or rose-water, and sufficient sugar. Butter a dish or basin; well mix your pudding; put it into the dish, and bake or boil it forty minutes. If baked, you may put a little cream upon the top.

CRIT TARTS.

Take half a pound of crit, which is the brown fat remaining after you have melted down your flay to make hogs'-lard, add a quarter of a pound each of cleaned currants, chopped apples, rice swelled in milk, enough sugar to your taste, a grated nutmeg, and a tablespoonful of ginger in powder. Mix all together, line

some patty-pans with a puff-paste, lay in some of the mixture, cover with a crust, and bake; and serve as you would
mince pies.

ZOUAVE PUDDING.

Put one good-sized clove of garlic into a quart of milk; set the
milk upon a slow fire or in a gentle oven, and let it reduce until it
is a custard. Remove the garlic, add the yolks of four well-beaten
eggs, a gill of rum, and two ounces of pounded loaf-sugar; butter
a dish, pour in your pudding, and bake for half an hour. This is
equal to any almond pudding ever made.

NOVEMBER.

THE only thing that tends to brighten this, the dullest of all dull months, is the coming in of the Christmas fruits. We can now reasonably calculate upon having our hunters' puddings and our mince pies—though if we think it unorthodox to anticipate the proper period for the latter dish, we can reconcile ourselves to indulging in it under the disguise of a rolled pudding à la Chateaubriand or a St. Martin's tart, for we have the Feast of Martinmas to keep, and, after all, mincemeat is not so very dear, albeit we are so chary of it; at the present price of raisins and currants an exceedingly good mincemeat may be made in the following manner, at a cost of about eightpence a pound:—

MINCEMEAT.

One pound of beef-suet, one pound of currants washed very clean in two or three waters and dried before the fire, a pound of raisins stoned and cut up, a pound of sultana raisins, a quarter of a pound of candied-peel, two pounds of minced apples, one pound of moist sugar, the juice of two lemons, and their rinds pared off as thin as possible and shred small, a quarter of a pound of mixed spice, and a gill of brandy.

PUDDINGS, ETC., FOR NOVEMBER.

Semolina Pudding.
Sunderland Puddings.
Plain Suet Pudding, baked.
Ginger Tart.
Soufflé Pudding.
Cumberland Pudding.
Ground Rice Pudding, boiled.
Carrot Pudding, boiled.
Martinmas Pudding or Tart.
Pith Pudding.
Hunters' Pudding.
A Grateful Pudding.

Rolled Pudding à la Chateaubriand.
Quince Pudding.
Arrowroot Pudding.
Oxford Puddings.
Cocoa-nut Cheesecakes.
Pudding aux Amandes.
Rich Marrow Pudding.
Pistachio Pudding.
Normandy Pippin Pudding.
The Cardigan Pudding.
Orange Pudding, boiled.
Lemon Flummery.

SEMOLINA PUDDING.

Boil a pint of milk and gradually stir in enough semolina to thicken it sufficiently; add some loaf-sugar, the beaten yolks of six eggs, and a spoonful of orange-flower water; then whisk the whites of four eggs to a cream, stir them into the pudding; take a mould, butter it well, and dust it thickly over with sifted bread-crumbs and pounded sugar. Pour in the ingredients, put it into a quick oven, bake for half an hour, turn into a dish, and serve.

SUNDERLAND PUDDINGS.

Beat the yolks of four eggs and the whites of three; mix them with half a pint of cream, a little laurel-water, and nutmeg and sugar; add enough flour to form a light paste. Beat all well together; butter small cups, half fill them with the pudding, and bake for thirty minutes. Turn them into a dish to serve, and pour wine sauce over them.

PLAIN SUET PUDDING, BAKED.

Take a pint of milk; gradually stir in half a pound of flour, six ounces of chopped suet, two eggs, four ounces of sliced candied citron-peel, four ounces of sugar, and a little spice. Bake it in a buttered mould for an hour in a gentle oven, and turn it into a dish to serve.

GINGER TART.

Peel and core half a dozen Ribston-pippins; cut them into long thin slices, and place them in a very slow oven to shrivel; when they feel limp and tough, take them out, lay them in a pie-dish with plenty of sugar, and pour over them a good tablespoonful of extract of ginger, or if it can be procured, half a bottle of Oxley's tincture of ginger. Let them stand an hour or so to absorb; stir them up occasionally; edge the dish with a rim of paste, cover with a top crust, and bake in a slow oven for an hour.

SOUFFLÉ PUDDING.

Take half a pound each of butter and flour, the beaten yolks of six eggs, a quarter of a pound of sifted loaf-sugar, and two dessert-spoonsful of orange-flower water. Beat all together for a quarter of an hour, then whisk the whites of the eggs to a froth and add them to the other ingredients. Put it into a buttered mould and boil it for an hour, or bake it for forty minutes. Serve with sifted sugar on it.

CUMBERLAND PUDDING.

Take half a pound of apple pulp or grated apples, six ounces of currants, six ounces of chopped suet, six ounces of flour, six eggs, and grated nutmeg and sugar to taste. Mix the whole well together, put it into a floured cloth, and boil for two hours. Serve with wine sauce poured over it.

GROUND RICE PUDDING, BOILED.

Take four ounces of blanched sweet-almonds; rub a bit of butter over a frying-pan; get it very hot; put in your almonds and shake them about until they are nicely browned; then put two ounces of rice into half a pint of milk; stir it over the fire until it is very thick; then withdraw it and mix in half a pint of cream, the parched almonds, two ounces of sugar, the beaten yolks of six eggs and the whites of three; boil it in a buttered mould for one hour. Serve with orange or lemon sauce.

CARROT PUDDING, BOILED.

Take eight ounces each of flour, washed currants, beef-suet, and carrots boiled and mashed smooth, some spice and sugar. Boil it for three hours in a basin; turn it out, and serve with wine sauce.

MARTINMAS PUDDING OR TART.

Boil a quarter of a pound of whole rice in milk; when done, drain it, and add a quarter of a pint of cream, a pound of mincemeat, and four well-beaten eggs. Mix the whole together; butter a mould, and then dust it over with sifted bread-crumbs, put in your pudding and bake for forty minutes. Turn it into a dish

when done. If boiled, tie it in a floured cloth and dress it an hour.
Serve with burnt brandy.

PITH PUDDING.

Take a sufficient quantity of the pith of an ox; soak it in water for
a night; then free it from the skin, and beat it with a little orange-
flower water until quite smooth: then scald half a pint each of
new milk and cream; pour them upon a quarter of a pound of
blanched and beaten almonds, a tablespoonful of grated bread;
add this to the pith; sugar it to taste, and stir in the yolks of three
eggs and the whites of two. Line a dish with a puff-paste; lay in
your pudding, put some pieces of butter on the top and bake it
for an hour in a moderate oven.

HUNTERS' PUDDING.

Beat six eggs; mix them with half a pint of cream, a gill of
brandy, and half a pound each of chopped beef-suet, washed
currants and stoned raisins, two ounces of sugar, half a grated
nutmeg, and one ounce each of candied citron and orange peel.
Mix the whole well together; tie it in a cloth, and boil it three
hours.

A GRATEFUL PUDDING.

Take half a pound each of bread-crumbs and dry flour, then beat the yolks of four eggs and the whites of two; mix them with half a pint of new milk; stir in the bread and flour; add half a pound of stoned raisins, half a pound of washed currants, a quarter of a pound of sugar, and a large spoonful of ground ginger. Mix thoroughly together, and either bake it for three-quarters of an hour, or boil it for an hour and a half.

ROLLED PUDDING À LA CHATEAUBRIAND.

Make a very rich puff-paste, roll it out rather thin, spread it over with a layer of mincemeat, roll it up, fasten it together securely, and bake for forty minutes. Sift sugar over it, and serve as hot as possible.

QUINCE PUDDING.

Throw your quinces whole into water, simmer them gently until they are tender, then peel and scrape off the soft pulp; mix it with sugar. To a quart of pulp put a pint of cream and the beaten yolks of four eggs; stir it in with your quinces; butter a dish, pour in the pudding, and bake it half an hour. Or you may line a pudding basin with a thin crust, fill it with the fruit, etc., and cover it with a top crust: boil it for an hour.

ARROWROOT PUDDING.

Boil a good-sized stick of vanilla in a pint of new milk, then remove the vanilla, stir in a large spoonful of arrowroot, first mixed smooth with a little cold water; stir it over the fire until it is thick enough; sweeten it; add the yolks of four eggs and the whites of two. Line the edge of a buttered tart-dish with a rim of paste; put in the pudding; pour a little cream upon the top, and bake it for half an hour.

OXFORD PUDDINGS.

Wash four ounces of currants, add four ounces of finely-grated biscuits, four ounces of shred suet, a dessert-spoonful of powdered sugar, and some nutmeg; mix all well together with the yolks of three eggs; shape them into balls of the size of turkey-eggs, and fry them nicely brown.

COCOA-NUT CHEESECAKES.

Take half a pint of grated cocoa-nut, mix it with the yolks of four eggs, a glass of brandy, and half a pint of cream. Stir it over the fire to thicken it. Line your patty-pans with paste, lay in the cocoa-nut, and bake as you would small tarts.

PUDDING AUX AMANDES.

Pound two ounces of blanched almonds in a mortar, add two ounces of fresh butter, two dessert-spoonfuls of white wine, one of cream, one of orange-flower water, one of sugar, two eggs, and two ounces of potato flour. Beat all well together until it froths. Put it into a buttered mould, lay it in a quick oven, and serve as soon as it is well browned.

RICH MARROW PUDDING.

Well butter a pudding-mould and strew it thickly with bread-crumbs. Take some cream, beaten eggs, and sugar, and make a custard; then slice a pound of marrow, clean half a pound of currants, and grate half a pound of bread; put a layer of bread into your mould, then a layer of marrow, then some currants, then some of the custard; proceed thus until you have put in all your ingredients, cover with a very well-floured cloth, tie it down, and boil it an hour. Strew sugar over it to serve.

PISTACHIO PUDDING.

Put eight ounces of Pistachio-nuts into a mortar; pound them to a paste; add a little milk, a quarter of a pound of powdered loaf-sugar, half a pint of cream, two eggs, two dessert-spoonsful of rose-water, and four ounces of sultana raisins previously plumped in brandy. Boil it in a buttered mould for forty minutes. Serve with almond sauce.

NORMANDY PIPPIN PUDDING.

Put six or eight Normandy pippins into a tart-dish, quite cover them with cider, strew in a good deal of sugar, and place them over-night in a very slow oven. The next day they should be found to be nicely swelled, and have absorbed the cider. Put more sugar to them, place an edge of crust round the dish, make a rich custard, pour it over the apples, and bake for half an hour in a quick oven.

THE CARDIGAN PUDDING.

Stir four spoonsful of flour into a pint of raw milk, mix it very smooth. Beat together the yolks of four eggs and the whites of three, and a dessert-spoonful of noyeau, then add the milk and flour; beat it well for half an hour, put it into a buttered basin, and boil it for one hour and twenty minutes. Serve with wine sauce.

ORANGE PUDDING, BOILED.

Take six ounces of bread-crumbs, squeeze over it the juice of four oranges; add the grated rind of two oranges, and sugar it to your taste; mix it with a glass of brandy and the yolks of four eggs and the whites of two; put it into a buttered basin, and boil it for an hour. Serve with a spice sauce poured over it.

LEMON FLUMMERY.

Boil one ounce of the best isinglass in rather less than a pint of water; when completely dissolved, add the yolks of four eggs, four ounces of white sugar, and the juice of a lemon. Boil all together, then strain it into a basin, stirring it constantly until cool; add white wine to your taste; put it into your mould, and let it set. Turn it into a dish to serve.

DECEMBER.

ONE of the peculiarities connected with Christmas is the sublime resignation we show in respect to the expense of eggs. When these were comparatively plentiful, it was wonderful how assiduously we experimented to avoid using them; how we begrudged ourselves a batter pudding; how uncomplainingly we put up with a pancake entirely devoid of them; how contentedly we abstained from our accustomed custard, and when we had one it was a miserable contrivance, because eggs happened to be a shilling a dozen; but at Yule-tide, when they are often double that price, we evince the grandest indifference to their costliness, and not only use them in everything, but persist in using them extravagantly, just as though the aim of a whole twelvemonth's economy was for the sake of allowing ourselves the exercise of wicked prodigality upon that jovial time which comes but once a year. Now there is no need to be improvident in our employment of eggs. Epicures in times gone by did very well without them at this season when they were so dear, and in the composition of their plum porridge, that famous old forerunner of our Christmas pudding, eggs were not thought of; so, being only a modern innovation, they should be introduced moderately and diffidently instead of being ostentatiously intruded upon the other ingredients of a dish that in olden time was above being associated with so humble an accessory to its excellence as paltry "pullet's sperm."

As a rule, one egg to every pound and a half of pudding will be found sufficient.

PUDDINGS, ETC., FOR DECEMBER.

Macaroni Pudding, boiled.
The Rochdale Pudding.
St. Helena Pudding.
Cocoa-nut Pudding.
Richmond Pudding.
The Shrewsbury Pudding.
Lemon Custard Tart.
Date Pudding, boiled.
Snow Pancakes.
Spanish Pudding.
Almond and Raisin Pudding.
Saloop Pudding.

Christmas Pudding.
New Cabinet Pudding.
Sweet-Orange Pudding, baked.
Impromptu Pudding.
Apple Tart.
Lemon and Almond Pudding.
Mince Pies and Jam Tarts.
Vermicelli Pudding, baked.
The Home Pudding.
Potato Pie.
Apple Charlotte.
Omelette au Rhum.

MACARONI PUDDING, BOILED.

Break four ounces of macaroni into short lengths; put it into a saucepan with a quart of new milk and four ounces of powdered loaf-sugar; simmer it until it is quite tender: let it grow cold; then beat the yolks of six eggs and the whites of two; add them to the macaroni, with two tablespoonsful of cream, and an ounce of candied orange-peel cut into small slices. Put it into a buttered basin; cover with a floured cloth, and boil for an hour. Serve with a sultana or a saffron sauce.

THE ROCHDALE PUDDING.

Take a quarter of a pound of mincemeat, the same as used for mince pies, a quarter of a pound of mashed potatoes, a quarter of a pound of hard-boiled eggs chopped small, a quarter of a pound of butter melted, a quarter of a pound of blanched almonds bruised, and two eggs beaten up in a glass of French brandy. Mix all well together; put it into a pudding-mould and boil for two hours. Serve smothered in white sugar.

ST. HELENA PUDDING.

Cut some rather thin slices of white bread without crust; divide them into the size of small sippets; butter them on both sides, and fry them of a nice brown colour; then dip them into brandy: pack them into a buttered pie-dish, strewing a few currants and lemon-peel between. Pour in a quart of new milk in which you have beaten two eggs; add some sugar; let it stand two hours to soak, then bake it for forty minutes in a moderate oven. Serve, decorated with citron-chips on the top.

COCOA-NUT PUDDING.

Take half a pound of grated cocoa-nut and a quarter of a pound of blanched and beaten Brazil-nuts; throw them into a pint of boiling milk, and let them stay till cold. Then beat two eggs, two ounces of sugar, two ounces of cream, and a glass of brandy; mix in the other ingredients; put it into a tart-dish edged with a rim of puff-paste, and bake for half an hour.

RICHMOND PUDDING.

Take one pound of chopped suet, one pound of Muscatel raisins, stemmed but not stoned, one glass of Malaga wine, four ounces of flour, four ounces of brown sugar, half a nutmeg, and three eggs: mix well, and boil in a cloth for three hours.

THE SHREWSBURY PUDDING.

Take half a pound of dressed and peeled beetroot; pound it in a mortar till quite smooth, add a quarter of a pound of fresh butter, six ounces of loaf-sugar in powder, the juice of two lemons, and the grated rind of one, two penny sponge-cakes, a glass of brandy, and three eggs: beat these ingredients perfectly well together; put them into a buttered mould dusted over with bread-crumbs, and either bake for forty minutes or boil it for an hour.

LEMON CUSTARD TART.

Squeeze the juice of two lemons upon half a pound of loaf-sugar; then pare the rind as thin as possible, and put it with the sugar. Boil the rest of the lemons in a good deal of water until quite tender; beat and rub them through a sieve; add them to the other ingredients; pour in half a pint of white wine; let it simmer by the fire for an hour; then gradually mix it with the beaten yolks of four eggs and the whites of two; strain it into a tart-dish edged with a rim of puff-paste, and bake for twenty minutes.

DATE PUDDING, BOILED.

Soak six sponge-cakes in sufficient cream to moisten them; then take four ounces of fresh dates freed from their stones, cut them into thin slices lengthwise; add them to the sponge-cakes with two eggs, a little grated lemon-peel, and two ounces of pounded loaf-sugar. Mix the whole together; put it into a buttered basin, and boil it for an hour and a half.

SNOW PANCAKES.

When the snow is on the ground it may be advantageously employed for pancakes instead of eggs. Take four dessert-spoonsful of flour and two of snow, mix well together; then add enough cold water to make it into a very stiff batter. Fry quickly in boiling friture, and serve hot with spiced sugar and lemon-juice.

SPANISH PUDDING.

Take a quarter of a pound of fresh butter, a quarter of a pound of flour, and half a pound of blanched almonds beaten to a paste; add the white of an egg and a little cream; work it well together, and roll it out flat as for a rolled pudding; then lay upon the surface six ounces of either preserved apricot, pine-apple, or strawberry jam. Roll it up, fasten the edges together, and boil it for forty minutes tied in a floured cloth. Serve with saffron sauce poured over it.

ALMOND AND RAISIN PUDDING.

Chop half a pound of veal-suet; pick over half a pound of sultana raisins, and cut half a pound of blanched almonds into quarters; stir all together; add a glass of white wine, a grated biscuit, the juice of an orange, two ounces of powdered loaf-sugar, and three well-beaten eggs: mix thoroughly; put it into a cloth or basin and boil for two hours. Turn out, and serve with almond sauce in the dish.

SALOOP PUDDING.

Boil a pint of new milk, then mix two ounces of saloop powder with a dessert-spoonful of peach-water and two ounces of sugar: stir it into the milk; let it thicken over the fire; add two ounces of butter, and when it is cool, beat in it two eggs. Put it into a tart-dish edged with paste, and bake it half an hour.

CHRISTMAS PUDDING.

One pound of chopped beef-suet, one pound of stoned raisins, one pound of washed currants, half a pound of bread-crumbs, a quarter of a pound of sugar, half an ounce of mixed spice, a quarter of a pound of candied lemon and orange peel, a gill of brandy, a gill of cream, four eggs well beaten. Mix thoroughly and boil in a cloth for four hours. Serve with wine sauce or burnt brandy.

NEW CABINET PUDDING.

Take one ounce of sponge-cake, three ounces of macaroons, and one ounce of ratafia cakes. Stone a few raisins, stick them inside a buttered mould; place in the cakes in alternate layers over the sides of the mould; make a custard with half a pint of boiled milk, three eggs, and a little sugar; pour it over the cakes, fasten it carefully with a floured cloth so as to exclude the water, and boil it half an hour.

SWEET-ORANGE PUDDING, BAKED.

Well beat together four eggs, a quarter of a pound of butter, the juice of four sweet oranges, and the grated rind of one; add four ounces of sugar, a gill of white wine, and sufficient grated biscuit to make it a light batter. Line a tart-dish with a puff-paste, lay in your pudding, and bake for half an hour.

IMPROMPTU PUDDING.

Break up six sponge-cakes; soak them in sherry, then beat them up in two eggs, two ounces of pounded loaf-sugar, two ounces of sliced almonds, two ounces of shred candied citron-peel, and a teaspoonful of cream; put it into a buttered basin and boil it a quarter of an hour. Serve with a Downshire or ginger sauce.

APPLE TART.

Put a good puff-paste round the edge of your dish; pare, core, and cut up some good baking-apples; strew them over with sugar; lay them in your dish, interspersing them with a few spoonsful of preserved quince; cover with an upper crust, and bake it for an hour.

LEMON AND ALMOND PUDDING.

Blanch and beat to a paste half a pound of sweet-almonds; add enough orange-flower water to moisten it, then put in the juice of two lemons, the grated rind of one, a quarter of a pound of fresh butter, six ounces of powdered loaf-sugar, and four eggs, the yolks and whites beaten separately in a tablespoonful of cream. Work all well together; put it into a dish lined with a puff-paste, and bake it for half an hour.

MINCE PIES AND JAM TARTS.

These may be had throughout the year, if your mincemeat is made so as to keep well. Line patty-pans or tart-dishes with a rich puff-paste; lay in sufficient mincemeat or preserve; cover with a top crust, and serve hot or cold. If the jam you intend to use is highly preserved, it may be placed in the patty-pans after the paste is baked. Some tarts are only decorated with orna-mental strips of paste on the top, or are left without a top crust.

VERMICELLI PUDDING, BAKED.

Break up two ounces of Italian vermicelli; throw it into boiling water; let it stand five minutes, then drain it; squeeze over it the juice of a lemon; add half the rind grated, a quarter of a pound of powdered loaf-sugar, half a pound of chopped beef-marrow, two eggs, and a little nutmeg. Put it into a buttered dish, and bake for half an hour.

THE HOME PUDDING.

Take three-quarters of a pound of sultana raisins, a quarter of a pound of boiled carrot cut up small, but not minced, a quarter of a pound of currants washed and dried, a quarter of a pound each of flour and pounded biscuit, three-quarters of a pound of suet chopped fine, half an ounce of ground-ginger, the shred rind of half a lemon, two eggs, a teacupful of milk, and a mealy potato mashed smooth. Mix all thoroughly together, and boil in a mould for four hours and a half.

POTATO PIE.

Cut a pound of cold potatoes into quarters, halve these again, put them into a frying-pan of boiling butter, and shake them over the fire until they are nicely browned; then take them up, well sugar them, add to them a pound of stoned raisins, four ounces of bread-crumbs, half a pound of chopped suet, and three spoonsful of spice. Stir all well together, put it into a pie-dish edged with paste, throw in a little sugar, and pour over it a custard made with three eggs beaten up in half a pint of new milk and a tablespoonful of orange-flower water: put on a top crust, and bake for forty minutes.

APPLE CHARLOTTE.

Lay some thin slices of bread over the inside of a buttered mould; then fill it with apple marmalade or preserved fruit of any kind, place more bread upon the top, put it into a pretty hot oven, and bake for half an hour. Turn it out upon a dish to serve.

OMELETTE AU RHUM.

Well beat four eggs, add two ounces of pounded and sifted loaf-sugar, and two ounces of currants washed, dried in a cloth, and plumped in brandy. Put it into a pan of boiling friture, fry it, and serve with a glass of rum poured over it: set fire to the rum, and send it to table, flaming.

PUDDING SAUCES.

ALMOND SAUCE.

Blanch and beat smooth two ounces of sweet-almonds; throw upon them half a pint of boiling milk; strain it; add a dessert-spoonful each of orange-flower water and powdered loaf-sugar, and the beaten yolks of two eggs. Stir it over the fire until it is quite hot, but not boiling.

THE DOWNSHIRE SAUCE.

Boil a bruised laurel-leaf in a teacupful of water for five minutes; then remove the leaf, and add to the water two ounces of fresh butter, two ounces of veal-suet minced fine, two ounces of sugar, and sufficient potato-flour to add consistency to it. Before serving stir in a dessert-spoonful of eau-de-vie de Dantzic.

GINGER SAUCE.

Make half a pint of very good melted butter, using water instead of milk: the moment before serving, add half an ounce of powdered and sifted ginger, the juice of half a lemon, and two ounces of white sugar. Note—all sauces should be sent to the table as hot as possible.

SWEET EGG SAUCE.

Put the yolks of four hard-boiled eggs into a mortar with an equal weight of fresh butter and sugar; beat it smooth, then dilute it with a sufficiency of either milk or white wine as agreeable: add the grated rind of half a lemon; give it a boil, and serve.

EGG SAUCE À L'ORDINAIRE.

Lightly chop two hard-boiled eggs, and mix them with half a pint of melted butter; sweeten to the taste.

SAUCE AU VIN.

Pour half a pint of wine upon the yolks of three eggs; beat it together for ten minutes; add sugar, grated lemon-peel, and cinnamon to your taste. Warm it, but do not let it come to a boil.

COMMON PUDDING OR SWEET SAUCE.

This is merely equal quantities of wine, most generally white wine, and sugar, added to some very rich melted butter. Brandy is often substituted for the wine.

JAM SAUCE.

Take two good dessert-spoonsful of jam; stir it over the fire in a glazed saucepan until pretty hot, then add two ounces of fresh butter and a tablespoonful of brandy, wine, cider, or grape-juice: when the butter is melted, serve.

CURRANT SAUCE.

Put a dessert-spoonful of cleaned and dried currants, a dessert-spoonful of brandy, and a dessert-spoonful of sugar into half a pint of thick melted butter; stir it over the fire until quite hot.

CIDER SAUCE.

Simmer down a pint of cider and a quarter of a pound of loaf-sugar until it is quite a syrup; then put in two ounces of fresh butter, and when this is melted, serve.

SULTANA SAUCE.

Put two dessert-spoonsful of water into a small saucepan: when it boils, add a quarter of a pound of butter; stir it round and round one way until the butter is melted; then put in two ounces of sultana raisins that have been swelled in brandy, and serve immediately.

SPICE SAUCE.

Into some sweetened melted butter stir in some sifted ginger, and a teaspoonful each of bruised, but not powdered, allspice and beaten cinnamon.

RED WINE SAUCE.

Simmer half a pint of red wine, and a quarter of a pound of loaf-sugar, until the quantity is greatly reduced. Claret or home-made wine will do for this sauce.

SAFFRON SAUCE.

Make a strong infusion of saffron in a breakfast-cupful of milk; stir it over the fire with two ounces of butter rubbed in flour, one ounce of blanched sweet-almonds slightly chopped, a little cinnamon, and two ounces of white sugar. When well thickened, serve it.

ORANGE SAUCE.

Rub together two ounces of butter and one ounce of flour; then put it into a saucepan with the juice of four oranges, the shred rind of half a one, and two dessert-spoonsful of loaf-sugar. When the butter is melted, it is done.

WHITE SAUCE.

Take a gill of white wine, some loaf-sugar, and the whites of three eggs; beat them over the fire until they form a high froth, and serve immediately.

Red wine may be used when a coloured sauce is desired.

LEMON SAUCE.

Make some melted butter with water instead of milk: then put in two ounces of sugar, the juice and shred rind of half a lemon, and the other half freed from its skin, sliced thin, and each slice cut into quarters: give it a boil up, and serve.

SPICED SUGAR FOR FRITTERS, ETC.

This is simply one dessert-spoonful of very finely-powdered and sifted mixed spice mixed with three dessert-spoonsful of powdered sugar.

BURNT BRANDY FOR PUDDINGS, ETC.

Put four large nubs of loaf-sugar into a saucer with a gill of pale brandy; set fire to the sugar, and directly it is dissolved, serve it over the dish intended.

ADDENDA.
FOR ALL SEASONS.

CUSTARD PUDDINGS, WITH DAMSON SYRUP.

Make a very good custard. To five eggs put half a quarter of an ounce of isinglass. Put the above in little dariole-moulds in a cool place till quite cold; then put them in warm water, to make them turn out of the moulds. After you have set them on the dish, pour round them damson or currant juice, perfectly sweetened. They ought to stand quite steady.

CAKE PUDDING.

Three eggs, their weight in sugar, flour, and butter, a little grated rind of lemon. Whip the eggs up separately, then the butter to a cream, stir in the flour gently and mix all well together. Butter the cups, and bake them twenty minutes.

ITALIAN CHEESE.

To a pint of thick cream, whipped very smooth, add the juice of three lemons, and the rind of two. Sugar to taste. Let it stand for half an hour, then whip it till very thick; tie it in a thin cloth, or a tin with holes in it. Let it stay and dry till next day; then turn out.

GATEAU DE POMMES.

Take half a pound of lump-sugar, put it to half a pint of water; let it boil till quite dissolved, and ready to candy: then add one pound of apples, pared and cored, and the peel of half a lemon. Boil it together till it is quite stiff; then put it into a mould, and when it is cold, it will turn out. Serve it with thick custard round it.

HALF-PAY PUDDING.

Suet, flour, currants, raisins, bread-crumbs, a quarter of a pound of each, neither more nor less.

Add two tablespoonsful of treacle and half a pint of milk; all which must be well mixed together, and boiled in a mould for three hours. Serve with wine or brandy sauce.

NEWCASTLE PUDDING.

Butter a basin or mould; stick it all round with raisins or dried cherries; then put in a slice of bread soaked in milk, and over that, layers of thin bread, buttered, until three-parts filled. Fill up with custard, and boil for an hour and a half.

VANILLA CREAM.

Boil half a stick of vanilla in a quarter of a pint of new milk, until highly flavoured, and sweeten with sugar. Dissolve an ounce of isinglass in a pint of water, mix with the vanilla milk, and add a pint, or rather more, of good thick cream. Stir until nearly cold, and pour into a mould, previously dipped in cold water.

PERSIAN CREAM.

Dissolve gently one ounce of isinglass in a pint of new milk, and strain; then put it in a clean saucepan with three ounces of sugar broken small, and when it boils stir into it half a pint of good cream; add this liquid at first by spoonsful only to eight ounces of apricot or raspberry jam; mix them very smoothly, and stir the whole until it is nearly cold, that the jam may not sink to the bottom of the mould. When the liquid is put to the fruit and has been stirred till nearly cold, whisk them briskly together; and last of all, throw in by very small portions at a time the strained juice of a good lemon. Put it into a mould, and let it stand at least twelve hours in a cold place before turning out.

LEMON SPONGE.

Dissolve two ounces of isinglass in a pint of water, one pound of loaf-sugar, pounded, the juice of four lemons: whisk it to a froth; put it in a mould the day before wanted.

SPANISH CREAM.

Half a pint of cream, same of new milk, three ounces of rice flour, a tablespoonful of orange or peach-flower water; sweeten it to taste. Boil till it is stiff, stirring it constantly, and when it will leave the side of the pan, put it into a mould which has first been put in cold water.

PLUM PUDDING.

Equal quantities of flour, raisins, or currants, and sugar, made into a paste with water; boil three or four hours, the longer the better.

BATTER PUDDING.

Three large spoonsful of flour, two or three eggs; stir it up very smooth, mixing in by degrees half a pint of milk; it must boil an hour and a half.

ANGEL PUDDING.

Two ounces of flour, two ounces of sugar, one ounce of butter, half a pint of milk, the yolks of four eggs and whites of two; melt the butter in part of the milk, and when cold, mix the whole together. This quantity fills four cups. Bake them nearly half an hour; soft sugar and wine in dish.

FRIAR'S OMELETTE.

Stew eight apples as for sauce, then stir in two ounces of butter; sugar to your taste. When it is cold, add four eggs well beaten, a little lemon-peel, and if the apples are flat, a little cinnamon-juice. Stir it up all together; then take a baking-dish, butter the sides and bottom well; then thickly strew crumbs of bread all over it; then put in the apples, and strew crumbs of bread all over the top, and bake it. When baked, turn it out of the dish and serve it up with sugar sifted over it.

PUDDING.

Half a pound of flour, treacle and suet chopped fine, well mixed and boiled for six hours. Wine sauce.

ORANGE SPONGE.

Take the juice of five large oranges, one lemon, half a pound of sugar, one ounce of isinglass dissolved in half a pint of water; put the juice upon the rind of the fruit peeled thin, to remain four hours; then take out the peel; put the juice, sugar, and isinglass into a pan; make the mixture hot, but not to boil; strain it through muslin, and whisk it well until nearly cold; then put it into a mould that has been put into cold water. It takes a long time whipping. The juice of any fruit will do prepared exactly in the same way; saffron may be added to the orange sponge to improve the colour.

BOILED LEMON PUDDING.

Half a pound of suet chopped fine, half a pound of bread-crumbs, one large lemon or two small ones, grated; squeeze then in the juice to these ingredients, three eggs, six ounces of white sugar. Boil forty minutes.

RATAFIA PUDDING.

Quarter of a pound of ratafia cakes, two ounces of raisins, three-quarters of a pint of milk, the yolks of five eggs, sugar to taste, half a teaspoonful pounded of bitter almonds, and a little brandy. Good either baked or boiled.

NORTHUMBERLAND PUDDING.

One pint of milk, boiled; stir some flour in it till thick as hasty pudding; a little butter, quarter of a pound of currants, with a little brandy, nutmeg, four eggs, sweetened to taste. Put them in cups; bake, and serve with wine sauce.

DENTON PUDDING.

A teacup full of new milk, a gill of cream, one ounce of butter, two ounces of loaf-sugar, a small piece of lemon-peel; put it into a pint stewpan all together; let it boil; mix two large spoonsful of fine flour with a little milk; then mix it with the boiling milk; let it boil well up; then rub it through a colander, and when a little cold, put to it five yolks of eggs with two tablespoonsful of orange syrup; beat up the whites to a strong froth, and mix all together; butter a mould or basin rather thick, and flour it; steam it an hour, taking off the cover often; you must not put the cover close at first, as the pudding rises fast; it will require looking to every five minutes. It will not burst by taking the cover off a little way, and then putting it on again. Heat some good apricot jam, and pour over it when sent to table. The batter must be about as thick as good bread-sauce.

CARROT PUDDING.

Boil six carrots till tender; pound them in a mortar; then put a little flour, a bit of butter, a little cream, four eggs, sugar to your taste. Put them in little moulds to bake.

WAFERS TO EAT WITH ICE.

Take half a pound of flour and a quarter of a pound of sugar, two yolks of eggs, half a pint of new milk, and the rind of half a lemon grated; mix them. Bake them in the wafer tins (making them the proper heat first); roll them off the tins on a stick; then set them on their ends in a sieve on the stove to dry.

A TRIFLE.

Some sponge biscuits and macaroons soaked in white wine, a little preserve over them; then cover with a custard and whipped cream on the top.

NUNS' PUFFS.

Take half a pint of water, two ounces of butter, two ounces of sugar, and boil it in the water; then stir as much flour in as will make it stiff; when quite smooth, put in three eggs; then drop them in tins any size you like, and bake them.

APPLE PUFF.

Prepare some apples in the same way as for sauce; while hot beat them up with a small quantity of butter and a very little sugar; lemon-juice and sugar to taste. Take the whites of two eggs and beat them up with two spoonsful of wine, one of cream, one of pounded sugar, and one of lemon-juice; when beaten to a froth put it on the apples.

STRAWBERRY JELLY CREAM.

Pick and pass through a fine sieve a pint of very best strawberries, to which add the juice of a lemon, six ounces of powdered sugar, and an ounce and a half of melted isinglass (a sufficiency of calves'-feet jelly to set it); put the above ingredients into a bowl, keeping its contents stirred until upon the point of setting, then stir in three parts of a pint of cream, first whipped; fill your mould.

FRESH RASPBERRY OR STRAWBERRY CREAM.

A pint and a half of fresh fruit beaten with half a pound of loaf-sugar, and the juice of a lemon; stir to it a pint and a half of cream, or half that quantity of cream and half of new milk, putting the cream first. Beat it long till it bears a fine froth, and put it in glasses or in a glass dish.

FIG PUDDING.

Half a pound of figs finely chopped, half a pound of bread-crumbs, half a pound of suet, quarter of a pound of sugar, some lemon-peel, and three eggs; mix all together, the same as for plum-pudding, and boil it for two hours.

INDEX OF RECIPES.

PUDDING SAUCES, ETC.

ADDENDA FOR ALL SEASONS.

CONVERSION TABLES.

WEIGHT.

Imperial Pounds (lb) and Ounces (oz)	Metric Kilogrammes (kg) and Grammes (gm)
½ oz	10 gm
1 oz	25 gm
2 oz	50 gm
4 oz (quarter of a pound)	110 gm
6 oz	175 gm
8 oz (half a pound)	225 gm
10 oz	275 gm
12 oz	350 gm
14 oz	400 gm
1 lb	450 gm
2 lb	900 gm
3 lb	1.35 kg

VOLUME.

Measure	Imperial Fluid Ounces (fl oz)	Metric Litres and Millilitres (ml)
1 gallon (imperial)	160 fl oz	4.5 litres
1 quart (imperial)	40 fl oz	1.2 litres
1 pint (imperial)	20 fl oz	600 ml
1 breakfast cup	10 fl oz	300 ml
1 gill	5 fl oz	150 ml
1 teacup	5 fl oz	150 ml
1 tablespoon	⅝ fl oz	18 ml
1 dessertspoon	⅖ fl oz	12 ml
1 teaspoon	⅕ fl oz	6 ml
1 saltspoon	1/20 fl oz	1.5 ml

SPOONS.

Measure	Equivalent
Tablespoon	2 dessertspoons
Dessertspoon	2 teaspoons
Teaspoon	4 saltspoons
Saltspoon	¼ teaspoon

OVEN TEMPERATURES.

Description	Gas Mark	Electric Fahrenheit (°F) and Celsius (°C)
Very cool	¼	225°F (110°C)
	½	250°F (130°C)
Cool, gentle, slow	1	275°F (140°C)
	2	300°F (150°C)
Very moderate	3	325°F (170°C)
Moderate, gay, tolerably quick	4	350°F (180°C)
Moderately or fairly hot, pretty quick	5	375°F (190°C)
	6	400°F (200°C)
Hot	7	425°F (220°C)
	8	450°F (230°C)
Very hot	9	475°F (240°C)

These temperatures are only an approximate guide as all ovens vary slightly, according to the make and country of manufacture.

GLOSSARY.

————

This glossary has been included to aid the modern cook, who may not be familiar with some of the ingredients, methods or equipment used in this Victorian cookbook. In some cases, you might use this guide to seek out authentic ingredients in order to be true to the recipes; in others, you might use it to choose suitable substitutions.

bullace Variety of plum, similar to damson.

Carolina rice Variety of American long grain rice.

cocoa-nut Coconut.

codlin Variety of apple, used for cooking.

crit The brown fat remaining after you have melted down flay to make hogs'-lard.

eau-de-vie de Dantzic An eau-de-vie of lemon peel and mace.

flummery A sweet, gelatinous pudding.

friture The oil or fat for deep frying, batter for frying or the fried food itself.

Hollands (glass of) The juniper-flavoured traditional liqueur of the Netherlands and Belgium from which gin evolved. Also known as jenever or Dutch gin.

isinglass A substance obtained from the dried swim bladders of fish, used as you would use gelatine in jellies and other puddings.

laurel water Water infused with bay leaf.

laurel leaves Bay leaves.

May Duke cherry Variety of cherry.

mazzards Variety of cherry, small & black.

medlar A fruit. Looks like a cross between a small apple and rosehip.

Naples biscuits A small plain biscuit, similar to a ladyfinger.

noyeau An almond-flavoured liqueur made from apricot kernels.

Oxley's tincture of ginger A brand of concentrated ginger essence.

paste Pastry.

patty-pan A baking pan or tin similar to a muffin tin but with rounded bottoms (like patties).

peach water Water infused with peach.

penny-roll Cheap, everyday bread roll.

penny sponge-cake Small, basic sponge cake, similar to a ladyfinger.

pippin (Normandy, Ribston) Varieties of apple.

pith Bone marrow.

ratafia cake A light biscuit, risen by egg whites, very similar to a macaroon.

salamander A cast-iron plate that was heated and then held over food to grill or brown it.

tansy A flowering herb.

whortleberry A variety of berry, similar to a blueberry.

loaf sugar Sugar that was sold moulded into a solid conical shape and packaged in paper.

saloop A powder of ground Turkish orchid root and herbs, from which a traditional East Indian beverage was made.